Just Engaged

Prepare for Your Marriage
before You Say "**I Do**"

Christine E. Murray, Ph.D.

Aadamsmedia

Avon, Massachusetts

This book is dedicated, with love, to my husband,
Dr. Tom Murray

Published by
Adams Media, an F+W Publications Company
57 Littlefield Street, Avon, MA 02322. U.S.A.
www.adamsmedia.com

ISBN-10: 1-59869-329-8

ISBN-13: 978-1-59869-329-4

Printed in the United States of America.

J I H G F E D C B A

Library of Congress Cataloging-in-Publication Data
is available from the publisher.

This publication is designed to provide accurate and authoritative information with regard to
the subject matter covered. It is sold with the understanding that the publisher is not engaged
in rendering legal, accounting, or other professional advice. If legal advice or other expert
assistance is required, the services of a competent professional person should be sought.

—From a *Declaration of Principles* jointly adopted by a Committee of the
American Bar Association and a Committee of Publishers and Associations

Many of the designations used by manufacturers and sellers to distinguish their product are
claimed as trademarks. Where those designations appear in this book and Adams Media was
aware of a trademark claim, the designations have been printed with initial capital letters.

This book is available at quantity discounts for bulk purchases.
For information, please call 1-800-289-0963.

Contents

Acknowledgments

I am extremely grateful to the many people who helped bring this book to publication, as well as those who provided emotional support to me while I was working on it. First, I wish to thank my agent, Molly Lyons from the Joëlle Delbourgo Associates agency. I appreciate her encouragement, editorial suggestions, and commitment to bringing this book to press. I am also grateful to Jennifer Kushnier at Adams Media for her enthusiasm for this project.

This book is based on the research I did for my doctoral dissertation at the University of Florida. My dissertation committee was extremely supportive of my research, and they helped me to develop my research ideas more fully. I am grateful for the support of Drs. M. Harry Daniels, Silvia Echevarria-Doan, Millie Ferrer, and Ellen Amatea for their contributions as members of my committee. I owe a special word of thanks to my dissertation committee chairman, Dr. Peter A. D. Sherrard. I will always be grateful to him for his mentoring and encouragement, as well as for challenging me to grow professionally and personally throughout my graduate studies.

I also want to thank my colleagues in the Department of Counseling and Educational Development at UNCG for their continued support of my professional development. I am particularly indebted to my graduate research assistant at UNCG, Jennifer Graybeal, who played a key role in making the publication of this book possible.

I am so thankful to have the support of wonderful friends and family members. My parents, Leslie Ward and Michael and DiAnn Borasky, have always been positive sources of encouragement for me, and I appreciate them more every day. I want to thank my mother, in particular, for her willingness to read and provide feedback to me on earlier versions of this book. Thanks are also due to my brother, Alan Borasky, and sister, Jennifer Mitts, for their continued support. Although they are too numerous to name everyone individually, I have immense appreciation for all of the friends and family members in my life.

Finally, what book on relationships would be complete without an expression of my gratitude to my own partner—my husband, Tom Murray? Tom is my best friend, personal comedian, number one supporter, and true partner in every sense of the word. I appreciate everything that he brings into my life, and I hope that our marriage continues to grow stronger in the years to come.

Introduction

Congratulations! You found the person with whom you want to share the rest of your life! It is exciting, romantic, and, of course, somewhat scary to think about your future marriage. Before you get caught up in the frenzy that surrounds planning a wedding, consider *why* you are getting married. Most people want to get married so they can continue to share their love with their partner and grow within the strength of that relationship. Of course, you want your wedding day to be memorable. But my guess is that it is much more important to you to have a happy, long-lasting marriage.

This book helps you prepare for the initial adjustments to married life. I surveyed more than 200 providers of premarital counseling to find out the topics they think are essential for couples preparing for marriage to address. That research is the basis for this book, and you will find their expert guidance throughout these pages.

All premarital couples are unique. Every person who reads this book will experience this time differently. For this reason, I provide exercises and discussion questions to help you identify the most relevant areas to you and your partner. Begin with the first exercise at the end of this introduction, which will help you figure out which topics are most important for you and your future spouse to address and will help you determine how this book can be most helpful to you. Your marriage will be different from every other marriage that has ever existed, so prepare for it in a way that accounts for your partner's and your life experiences, personality characteristics, and dreams for the future.

You may discover some issues that could use further attention under the skilled guidance of a trained professional, and I urge you to seize all the opportunities you can to prepare for your marriage, such as face-to-face counseling. Many couples think counseling is only for people who have problems. However, it also helps you build on what is going well. Every couple has some positive and negative aspects to their relationship. Couples are only able to move forward in their relationships when they acknowledge that their relationships are not perfect. To help you decide on a premarital counselor, I include "A Consumer's Guide to Premarital Counseling" in Chapter 19.

I believe that marriage can be a wonderful, rewarding, life-altering experience. Marriage potentially brings many positive experiences into your life—the possibility of starting a new family, the security of knowing you are in a lifelong commitment, opportunities to grow as an individual, and the chance to share an ever-deepening love with your partner.

Marriage in Society

According to the U.S. Census Bureau, approximately 80 to 90 percent of American men and women marry during their lifetimes. Modern folklore contains many mixed messages about married life. First, we are told that marriage is part of the "American Dream," along with children, a home, and a satisfying career. This leads many people to believe that marriage brings guaranteed happiness and love. Unfortunately, single people are often assumed to be incomplete without a marital partner.

On the other hand, we hear that marriage brings boredom and misery. Images of nagging wives and emotionally unavailable husbands abound, as well as the common assumption that sexual relationships between spouses are boring and infrequent.

It is no wonder, then, that many expectations—positive and negative—surround the issue of marriage. Realistically, marriage can promise all of these things. In almost any marriage, there are times of sheer joy that would be impossible to achieve if not for the marital relationship. There are also times of disappointment, pain, and heartache that result from marriage. Ideally, the good times far outweigh the bad.

The Wedding Industry: Big Business for a Big Day

The wedding industry creates excitement and hype about the wedding celebration. Weddings are big business. The average wedding today costs more than $20,000, and many couples plan extravagant, luxurious weddings (whether they can afford them or not). In addition, many couples extend the lengths of their engagements, not to get to know one another better, but to plan the "perfect" wedding. It seems that the $40 to $80 billion industry that surrounds wedding planning spreads the message that the only prerequisite for a satisfying marriage is a beautiful wedding ceremony.

Wedding magazines can be both helpful and anxiety provoking. When I planned my wedding, I nearly had a panic attack the first time I looked through a bridal magazine! The magazine was full of schedules mandating when each step of the planning process should be complete (e.g., secure a location at least a year in advance, arrange for an officiant ten months before the ceremony, and buy a dress with sufficient time for alterations to be made). In my first glimpse through one such magazine, I realized I was already hopelessly behind schedule.

Wedding magazines can be helpful in reminding engaged couples of the steps needed to create a wedding, providing helpful hints for planning, showing wedding dresses, and providing honeymoon travel suggestions. However, these magazines are intended to help you plan your *wedding*, not your *marriage*. While they can be a helpful resource during your engagement, they should not be your only resource for preparing for marriage.

During your engagement, you have two separate, yet related, sets of plans to make. You must plan for your wedding, and you must plan for your marriage. Planning for the wedding provides practice for you in preparing for the marriage. Planning a wedding—large or small—involves many experiences that are similar to the challenges you face once you are married. For example, you may face financial decisions, big and small disagreements, times of stress, and the negotiation of relationships with your family-of-origin. These challenges provide rich opportunities to grow and strengthen your relationship.

Why Marriage?

Why do people get married, anyway? More important, why are *you* getting married? This is one of the questions I hope you will consider thoughtfully as you prepare to enter marriage. Couples marry for many reasons. Fortunately, there are no "right" or "wrong" reasons to marry, although some reasons are certainly more beneficial to the relationship than others. Many engaged individuals say, "I am getting married because I love my partner and want to spend the rest of my life with him/her." People also cite some of the following reasons for getting married:

- "I am at a point in my life where I am ready to settle down."

- "I want to start a family and have kids, and I think marriage is the best arrangement for doing so."

- "I want to have the legal privileges associated with marriage."

- "I have always wanted to get married."

- "Now just seems like the right time."

- "I hope that having that commitment will keep my partner from cheating on me (or stop the fighting, or help me to feel secure in my relationship)."

- "My partner offers me the security I have been looking for."

- "We want to live together, but our family won't accept it if we're not married."

- "I want to make sure I have someone to grow old with. I don't want to be alone."

- "My parents (friends, coworkers, siblings, etc.) think it is the best thing for me."

- "This is the one person I've dated with whom I can see myself spending the rest of my life."

Some of these reasons may seem surprising, and not all of them apply to every couple. Most people have several reasons for getting married. The reasons you are getting married shape your expectations and your experiences in marriage. Consider an individual whose primary reason for getting married is for the security he has found in his partner. His expectation is that life with his spouse will be comforting, safe, and stable. Imagine what would happen if his spouse were to announce a plan to make an extreme career change and request that he move across the country in pursuit of this new career. This request entails major lifestyle changes and could shatter the stability that this man expects from marriage. The marriage could survive these transitions, but this man would need to alter his expectations of his spouse to accommodate his wife's requests. Think about your reasons for wanting to get married, and discuss this issue with your partner.

Your Engagement Matters!

Researchers can predict which engaged couples will eventually divorce with accuracy rates of 77 to 90 percent. What does that tell us? First, your current relationship, and how you prepare for marriage, matters in what your relationship will be like years from now. Second, 10 to 23 percent of couples' relationships defy all odds. Some couples that seem to have healthy, happy relationships will ultimately break up. Some relationships that seem destined for failure survive. Although nearly all engaged couples have expectations of a happy, successful marriage, most enter marriage with keen awareness of a divorce rate that lingers above 50 percent. This book will help you develop skills and resources now that will help you when problems and disagreements arise in your marriage.

Make your relationship a priority in good and bad times. When you make your marriage a priority and share that commitment with your partner, you pay attention to the path your marriage takes. You have an honest assessment of the strengths and weaknesses of your relationship. You celebrate the successes of your relationship, and you enhance your relationship in the weak spots. You seek out help when needed. You appreciate your partner for who he or she is—flaws and all. The earlier you commit to prioritizing your relationship, the more likely you are to develop a solid foundation for your marriage. As you think about your upcoming marriage and your life together, prioritize your relationship and be sure to give it the attention it deserves.

Organization of This Book

This book explores issues to consider as you prepare for your marriage. In an effort to make this book applicable to both genders but keep it readable, I've alternated between chapters my use of male and female pronouns. The premarital counseling providers who participated in my study rated the importance of topics that are often addressed in premarital counseling and/or educational programs. Chapters 1 through 17 are arranged in the order of importance that providers ascribed to each topic. Because your relationship is unique, some issues providers rated as most important may be less relevant to you, while some issues providers rated as less important may be most salient in your relationship. Relationships change over time. Throughout your marriage, the topics in this book will vary in their degree of importance to you. Decide how much time to spend on each topic based on your needs.

Chapter 18 discusses the decision to end an engagement. Chapter 19 presents a Consumer's Guide to Premarital Counseling, including information to help you select a premarital counseling provider and program. Finally, the Conclusion summarizes the lessons contained in this book and reminds you of the exciting adventure on which you are about to embark.

Within many chapters, you will find case studies and discussion questions. The case studies, while based on composite experiences of real people, are fictional, and they represent common situations couples face. Within each chapter, you will also find a review section containing an Action Plan that you can apply to your relationship to address the topic of each chapter. Use the discussion questions throughout the book to promote individual reflection and discussion as a couple. I encourage you to go through this book together. Read and discuss one chapter at a time. Because you're probably very busy with your relationship, your wedding plans, and the rest of your life, I've made this book easy to use and interactive. I hope that this book will be a useful guide for you as you get ready for marriage!

Directions: How important is it to you to address the following topics before you get married? Rank the topics from one (most important) to seventeen (least important). Ask your partner to do the same. Then compare your rankings to see which topics are most important to you and your partner. Use this information to decide which chapters in this book require the most of your attention.

PARTNER A	PARTNER B

► Commitment to the marriage

_____   _____

► Communication

_____   _____

► Attitudes and beliefs about marriage

_____   _____

► Managing conflict

_____   _____

► Making time for each other

_____   _____

► Parenting and children

_____   _____

► Adjusting to married life

_____   _____

PARTNER A	PARTNER B
▶ The sexual relationship	
_____	_____
▶ Your values and dreams	
_____	_____
▶ Problem-solving and coping skills	
_____	_____
▶ Religion/spirituality	
_____	_____
▶ Gender role expectations/household tasks	
_____	_____
▶ Finances	
_____	_____
▶ Family-of-origin issues	
_____	_____
▶ Friendships and social support	
_____	_____
▶ Careers	
_____	_____
▶ Fun and leisure	
_____	_____

Dawn recently became engaged. She is excited to have found the love of her life. Dawn and her fiancé have many exciting plans for their future. They want two children and fulfilling careers, and someday they hope to retire to a beach community. Dawn and her fiancé are compatible in many ways. They share a love of music, cooking, and nature. Their relationship is built on these shared interests and a solid friendship.

Dawn feels ready to make the commitment involved in marriage. However, she cannot help but think about her parents' divorce. Her parents were unhappy in their marriage for many years before they finally divorced. Although Dawn remembers times when her parents seemed happy, she thinks back on the loud fights they had through the years. In truth, she was happy when they finally decided to divorce.

Now, Dawn thinks about her future marriage. She feels committed to making her marriage last, and she wants to avoid divorce at all costs. However, in the back of her mind, she thinks, "What would I do if my husband and I started to fight like my parents? I don't want to divorce, but I couldn't stay if my marriage was like theirs."

one

Commitment to Marriage

Divorce has become very common among modern families. In fact, marriages today are more likely to end in divorce than in the death of one spouse. The risk of divorce is highest in the early years of marriage, and the U.S. Census Bureau estimates that about one-quarter of all marriages end within seven years. Divorce can have many negative consequences for the spouses and their children, although researchers are beginning to identify some positive outcomes of divorce as well. Even when divorce is perceived as a positive change—such as when the marriage was filled with chronic, openly hostile conflict—the multiple transitions that arise through the divorce are likely to create a great deal of stress for everyone involved.

Dawn is like many people who grew up in a society in which divorce is common. Although she is excited about beginning her own marriage, she also knows that many marriages don't stand the test of time. It is natural for people like Dawn to have these mixed feelings as they prepare for marriage. Whether or not a divorce occurred in your own family, it is likely that you know a close friend, family member, coworker, or acquaintance who has experienced divorce. Not surprisingly, the widespread occurrence of divorce has changed the way many people think about the marital commitment. In one study, one-third of engaged couples expressed concerns about getting divorced. Witnessing, or being personally involved in, a divorce can lead a person to question his ability to maintain a long-term, committed relationship.

It is no surprise, then, that the premarital counselors I surveyed believe that the most important topic to address in premarital counseling is "commitment to the marriage." Many professionals who work with families express great concern over the costs of divorce to the individuals involved, as well as to the larger society. One premarital counselor stated, "I believe divorce is too easy to obtain and therefore allows the married couple an easy escape instead of working out their problems and situations. Marriage takes daily and total commitment to one another and the willingness to maintain a relationship." Another said, "We must do everything we can to reverse the horrendous divorce rate."

In an attempt to legislate marital commitment, some state governments implemented covenant marriage laws, which allow marrying couples to opt for a more rigorous legal commitment. For example, couples may be required to seek marriage counseling before they divorce. States in which these options exist at the time of this writing include Louisiana, Arizona, and Arkansas. State governments implemented these laws in an effort to enhance couples' marital commitments. However, at this time it remains unclear what effect measures like these will have on rates of divorce. Also, many couples either do not have options such as covenant marriages available to them, and many other couples would not choose to enter into such an arrangement. Therefore, most couples that marry are left to their own devices to grapple with commitment issues within their own marriages.

Commitment in Your Marriage

How can you address commitment in your relationship? A discussion about commitment to marriage once you are engaged may seem unnecessary. After all, haven't you already decided to remain faithful to your partner for the rest of your life? Doesn't an agreement to get married imply a high level of commitment

Directions: Answer the following questions with your partner. Follow the directions at the end to create a shared marital vision.

1. *What would you like to be happening in your marriage ten years from now?*

   PARTNER A _____

   PARTNER B _____

2. *What are your personal goals for your marriage?*

   PARTNER A _____

   PARTNER B _____

3. *How can you support your partner in reaching his/her goals for the marriage?*

   PARTNER A _____

   PARTNER B _____

4. *What would be your ideal balance between your marriage and other aspects of your life (e.g., your career, extended family, recreational interests, and friends)?*

   PARTNER A _____

   PARTNER B _____

5. *How would you like to describe the family you will create with your partner?*

   PARTNER A _____

   PARTNER B _____

Use your answers to the previous questions as a guide to create three specific goals for your future marriage. Create these goals together, and make sure that you both agree on them.

CONTINUED

Example: "We will have a happy, loving marriage." (*This is not specific enough. What does it mean to be happy? What does it mean to have a loving marriage?*)

Better Examples: "We will go on at least one date together each week." And "We will say, 'I love you' at least one time every day, even when we are fighting."

GOAL #1 _____

GOAL #2: _____

GOAL #3: _____

Now, using a separate piece of paper, create a Vision Statement for your own marriage. Be clear about this vision. This vision may take years to accomplish and may change, but you can begin now to make this vision a reality.

Example: "Our marriage will be a relationship in which we are both committed to the optimal well-being of ourselves and each other. We will support each other as best we can, by providing an ear for listening, a hand for holding, or encouraging words to lift a dampened spirit. We will be each other's best friends, and we will support each other in nurturing other relationships–such as with friends and family members. Our marital vision includes fun, laughter, love, and friendship. We will stand by one another in difficult times, and we commit to open communication and honesty in all things."

This Marital Vision Statement describes characteristics and specific behaviors. This statement provides a clear image of the marriage this couple wishes to have. Now, using a separate piece of paper, it's your turn to create a Vision Statement for your own marriage.

to your partner? What else could there be to discuss related to commitment? If only it were so simple. Commitment to marriage means more than remaining faithful to your spouse. Commitment means that you honor your relationship and your partner in all you do. You stand by your spouse and face the world together. This type of commitment does not require you to forsake your personal dreams, thoughts, and aspirations in favor of your partner's. Rather, full commitment to your relationship implies that you honor yourself as well, knowing that you must nurture your own growth in order to nurture your relationship. Partners who are committed to their marriages don't pick up and leave at the first sign of adversity. They work together with their spouses to manage the challenges they face. People express their commitment through their willingness to examine themselves and change those aspects of their character that do not help their relationships.

One of the most vital steps you and your future spouse can take to strengthen your commitment is to develop shared goals for your marriage. In other words, what do you want your relationship to be like over time? What type of marriage do you want to create with your partner? In addition to your individual goals for the relationship—such as changing your behaviors, supporting your spouse, or developing self-confidence—shared goals unite you with your partner. Together with your partner, build a mutually satisfying vision for your relationship, and establish a joint commitment to your future. When you develop goals, be specific. A couple who states a goal of "We want to have a happy marriage" does not have a specific goal. What does happiness mean to this couple and to each partner? A "happy marriage" means a lot of different things to different people. Details provide your vision with clarity. You can change your goals later as your life circumstances change—in fact, you can *expect* that your goals will change as you enter new stages of your relationship. Be courageous, and set goals that are positive and realistic. Complete Exercise 2 to develop marital goals and create a Marital Vision Statement.

Once you create your Marital Vision Statement, you will have a clear image of your aspirations for marriage. Keep your goals and Marital Vision Statement in a convenient, visible location. Copy them onto a separate piece of paper, and review them often. Once you are married, review your progress toward your goals and your vision to assess your continued commitment to marriage. If you discover that your marriage is no longer consistent with your goals or Vision Statement, you'll need to decide whether you've outgrown your goals and vision, or whether you've gone off track from what you hope to create in your marriage. Either way, maintain communication with your partner about your progress (which you'll read about more in the next chapter), and develop strategies to get your relationship back in line with your goals. These may include revising your original goals and Vision Statement based on your new circumstances, scheduling an appointment for couples counseling, or making changes in your daily lives to become more focused on your goals.

An Important Caution Related to Marital Commitment

You are committing to a relationship in which mutual respect and support are a primary goal. However, there are some situations in which unfaltering commitment to marriage is not in your best interest. For example, physical, emotional, verbal, and/ or sexual abuse occurs in some relationships. The consequences of these forms of abuse can be severe—including mental health problems, chronic injuries, financial consequences, and even death. Violence of any form is not acceptable. Commit first to your own safety and well-being. Marital violence is a serious problem, and there is a possibility that it will recur, especially if a violent partner does not receive treatment. Within a violent relationship, care for your own personal safety above your commitment to the relationship. Many resources are available to help if you are in this situation. Professionals who work with individuals who have experienced relationship violence—such as counselors, doctors, social workers, and the staff of domestic violence agencies—understand the complicated, often dangerous circumstances that can keep people who are being abused in their relationships. If you are ever in that situation, these professionals can provide a valuable source of support and information to you to help you determine the best steps to take in your situation.

Conclusion

We met Dawn at the beginning of this chapter, as she was struggling with some mixed emotions about her impending marriage. She was influenced in these thoughts by her parents' history and divorce, but there are a number of other reasons that you may experience similar feelings. Marriage is one of the biggest commitments you will make in your lifetime. As you prepare to marry, it is normal to question your own and your partner's commitment. Since you can't see into the future, you cannot know the circumstances that may arise and challenge your marital bond. Your life history and family background may have led you to question the durability of marriages in general, and particularly your own. Again, *these thoughts, doubts, and questions are a normal response to making an extremely important, life-changing decision.*

Spend time now thinking about the meaning of the commitment you will make when you marry. Both of you probably have some fears or concerns related to making such a significant commitment. Support each other in expressing these concerns by listening carefully and sharing your own concerns. Understand that your partner's (and your own) concerns probably do not reflect an inability to commit to your marriage. Rather, those questions and concerns are part of the process through which one must go in order to become committed fully to a life-long relationship. If you or your partner just can't seem to move beyond some of these questions or concerns, however, then it is probably wise to seek the guidance of a trusted mentor, a close friend, or a professional counselor. Those unshakable doubts could be signs that you have some serious concerns or issues related to your relationship, yourself, or your partner that you need to work on before getting married.

Commitment to marriage can be exciting, romantic, and anxiety provoking. Commitment provides the security and stability that are available through marriage. Commitment offers possibilities for life enhancement, personal growth, and constant love and support. However, if you focus on all of the other options that become unavailable to you once you marry, you may feel limited by such an intense commitment. As you consider your ability to commit to marriage, you become increasingly aware of the magnitude of the commitment you are about to make. Marriage is, indeed, a significant commitment, and one that has the potential to enrich your life greatly.

Action Plan: Commitment

1. Discuss what commitment means to you in your upcoming marriage.

2. Create shared relationship goals and a Marital Vision Statement. Review these often.

3. Remain committed to a relationship that is healthy, supportive, and respectful of both partners.

Discussion Questions

1. What does commitment mean to you?

2. Are there any situations in which you would be unable to remain committed to your marriage?

3. What do you think might be the biggest challenges to your marital commitment in years to come?

4. What did you learn about commitment to marriage growing up in your family?

5. What will you do to keep your commitment to the marriage strong, even during difficult times?

Susan is talkative, extroverted, and outgoing. Bob, on the other hand, is quiet, introverted, and a little shy. Even though they have different communication styles, Susan and Bob usually appreciate the sense of balance they provide for one another. In fact, Bob was attracted initially to Susan's bubbly, sociable personality, and Susan was attracted to Bob's calm, easygoing demeanor.

However, from time to time, the partners' different communication styles create stress in the their relationship.

two
Communication

Effective communication skills are essential to any healthy relationship. Strong communication skills allow us to understand our partners and our partners to understand us. Miscommunication is a common source of stress in all types of relationships, especially romantic relationships. The premarital counseling providers I surveyed indicated that it is very important for couples to consider their communication patterns before they marry. In addition, nearly all existing premarital counseling programs include a focus on communication skills. Improve the communication in your relationship by learning and practicing the communication skills that are most conducive to a positive relationship.

Even couples in satisfying, healthy relationships have communication mishaps from time to time. My husband, Tom, and I have come to refer to our communication mishaps as "miscommunication stations." This refers to those situations in which it becomes clear that we have been talking about two very different topics during a conversation. Unfortunately, we often don't realize we've arrived at the "station" until one or both of us experience a great deal of frustration and irritation with the other. Once we realize we've arrived, however, we slow down and backtrack until we're able to figure out when the misunderstanding began. We've never been unable to get back on track once we regrouped and moved forward—taking extra care to ensure that we're both talking about the same thing!

Communication within a marriage is challenging because of the constant proximity between spouses. It is difficult to be an effective communicator at all times, especially during stressful situations. Many people find it easy to use good communication skills when they are relaxed, but as soon as the tension rises, those skills seem to disappear. Therefore, couples can increase their chances of maintaining positive communication habits even during stressful times by learning to calm themselves down and by practicing effective communication strategies until those skills become second nature. In this chapter, I present four case studies to illustrate some common communication dilemmas for engaged couples. Along with these case studies, you will find strategies to enhance your communication within your relationship. These strategies address some of the essential communication skills required for maintaining a satisfying relationship.

Case Study #1: Susan and Bob

Let's return to Susan and Bob, the couple you met in the case study at the start of this chapter.

One day, Susan and Bob were discussing their wedding plans, trying to decide how many people to invite to the wedding. Susan listed all the people she wanted to invite, and the list grew longer by the minute. She became excited about all of her friends and family members who might come to the wedding, and the list continued to expand.

All of a sudden, Bob blurted, "Just stop! I don't want such a big wedding! I only want to invite a few guests, and certainly not as many as you're saying. This wedding is turning out to be exactly what I *don't* want!" He was noticeably upset, with an angry look on his face.

Susan was shocked by Bob's outburst, and she thought to herself, "He hasn't said anything about this before!"

What Can You Learn from This Example?

Susan and Bob's situation is common. Partners often are surprised when they do not agree on a particular issue. Susan perceived that Bob accepted her ideas about their wedding completely because Bob hadn't offered a different perspective. One reason these situations arise is because every person has a unique style of communicating. Partners have unique backgrounds, personalities, comfort levels, and habits—many of which they learned in their families of origin and through their peer groups. These experiences and characteristics shape communication styles, so no two people communicate in the same way. Communication within relationships is complicated by the differing meanings that partners ascribe to the words they use and conversations they have.

One way to understand Susan's and Bob's situation is to examine their different communication styles. The partners appear to process information differently. Susan is extroverted, while Bob is introverted. Extroverts and introverts have different ways of thinking and communicating. Extroverts tend to be more oriented toward people and things in the world around them, while introverts are more oriented to their own internal thoughts and dialogue. Although it is possible for an extrovert to be shy, most people who are extroverted process information best when they are talking about it aloud. Likewise, although an introvert can appear sociable, most people who are introverted process information in their mind before they speak. This distinction between "thinking aloud" and "thinking before you speak" is a major difference between Susan's and Bob's communication styles.

Susan, the extrovert, is talkative and animated while she speaks of their wedding plans. As Bob appears to be listening closely without saying much, she assumes he agrees with everything she says. Meanwhile, Bob pays attention to his own thoughts and processes them as they arise. As Susan talks, he becomes overwhelmed by her enthusiasm and feels that she is not concerned with his opinions about the wedding plans. He may even begin to feel resentful of Susan because she doesn't seem to notice his distress about the wedding plans. Bob's outburst surprises Susan, as they both understand the conversation differently.

Fortunately, people who have different communication styles can have satisfying relationships. Differences between partners can help keep a relationship exciting, and different communication styles can complement each other. In fact, partners with differing communication styles have a unique advantage in that their styles can provide balance to the dynamics within the relationships. An extroverted partner often appreciates having a sensitive partner to listen to her, and an introverted partner often appreciates that her extroverted partner helps to carry the conversation. Partners with similar communication styles face unique challenges of their own: two extroverted partners may feel that they need to work hard just to get one word into their conversations, and two introverted partners may experience frustration with limited amounts of verbal communication with their partners. Awareness of communication styles helps you communicate more effectively. The key is to identify your and your partner's preferred styles of communicating, and then figure out how you can best use those styles to enhance the communication patterns within your relationship.

Understand Your and Your Partner's Communication Styles

Become more aware of your own communication style and habits. Do this by observing what happens during your interactions, and reflecting later upon what you noticed during your observations. It can also be helpful to have talks with your partner about your communication, because it is likely that you will each notice different things. Pay particular attention to the areas in which you do well in communicating with each other, as well as the areas in which you could use some work. When you are aware of the strengths and weaknesses of your communication patterns, you can identify the areas in which you could make positive change. Also, learn about your partner's communication style. Is your partner introverted or extroverted? Is your partner's communication style similar or different to your own? How well does your partner's communication style complement your own? When you are sensitive to your partner's communication style, you are more likely to get your message across to your partner and to help your partner communicate most effectively with you.

If you are an extrovert and your partner is an introvert, ask more questions and involve your partner in the conversation. Be patient with your partner, and understand that she needs time to think before speaking. Be comfortable with silence. (This is not an easy task—it takes many of the counselor trainees I teach years before they can truly feel comfortable with silence, and they have special training in communication!) If you are introverted and your partner is extroverted, try to share more of your internal processes with your partner. Also, let your partner know when you need more time to think through an issue. Moments of miscommunication are normal. When you arrive at your own "miscommunication stations," step back, evaluate where you went off track, and try to progress further to your ultimate destination of an effective, respectful conversation.

Case Study #2: Aja and José

Aja and José are deciding on a budget for their wedding. Neither of their parents will be able to help with the wedding costs, so they'll have to cover all of the expenses themselves. They want to have a large wedding, because each partner has a big family.

However, they're not sure how much they'll be able to afford on their modest incomes. They also share other financial goals for the upcoming years, such as buying a house and saving enough money to be financially secure when they have children.

Right now, Aja and José are trying to decide how much money each is willing to take out of his or her savings account to put toward the wedding costs. José has significantly more money in savings than Aja, and he tells Aja, "I think we should go all out and have the best wedding we can afford. This is a one-time thing, and I want it to be really special."

Aja has a different approach. She says, "That's a really bad idea. I think we should try to cut costs and have a simple, inexpensive ceremony and reception. I don't think we can afford the type of wedding it sounds like you want to have. We should save our money for a down payment on a house in a couple years."

José replies angrily, "I thought this wedding was important to you. You want to cut corners—is that how you feel about our relationship? I can't believe you are being so cheap about our one and only wedding!"

What Can You Learn from This Example?

Aja and José are facing one of the many decisions involved in planning a wedding. A couple's communication during such decision points influences how effectively they can resolve the issue. Strong communication skills can help couples stay focused on the issue and find a resolution, whereas weaker communication skills can make a simple conversation turn quickly into a big fight. This is a really big decision for this couple. The amount of money they spend on their wedding will determine the number of people they can invite and the type of ceremony they will have, and the amount of money they have left in savings after the wedding will affect their future plans. In this brief exchange between Aja and José, we see that the couple is unlikely to resolve the issue peacefully if their discussion continues in this manner. Aja and José could improve their approach to this conversation by changing their communication patterns.

Aim for Understanding

After José tells Aja that he wants an expensive wedding, Aja disagrees immediately with him without giving José an opportunity to explain his reasons for desiring such a wedding. The couple appears to be viewing their wedding on two different levels: Aja is focusing on the practical issues, while José is focusing on the meaning of the wedding for their relationship. José's comments indicate that he believes the type of ceremony they have signifies their commitment to the relationship. Aja could have understood José's position more clearly by asking for clarification or by paraphrasing what she heard José say. She could say, "What is it about having a lavish wedding that is important to you?" Likewise, José could have done more to understand Aja's concerns about the couple's financial situation. For example, he could ask, "What are you most concerned about related to our finances and this wedding?" By asking questions such as these, Aja and José are more likely to understand one another's positions and avoid the reactivity that comes with jumping to conclusions about each partner's reasons for her opinions about their wedding finances.

Listen Actively

Both partners could have listened more carefully while the other one was talking. Active listening involves making an effort to listen to your partner, focusing on her message rather than planning what you will say next, and waiting patiently for your partner to finish. Because José did not listen actively to Aja, he jumped to the conclusion that Aja wanted to cut corners because she did not care about the relationship. By not seeking to understand Aja, José read more into Aja's statements than she intended, and he became unnecessarily angry. One strategy you can use to listen actively to your partner is to repeat back what she just said to you in your own words, and clarify whether you accurately heard the message. In this situation, José might say to Aja, "What I'm hearing you say is that having money for a house is more important than using our money for our wedding. Is that correct?" This question invites Aja to expand upon her initial statement and ensure that she is sending the message that she really wants to send to José.

Compromise

Aja and José's conversation is repairable. This couple needs to reach a compromise so they can resolve the larger issue of how much to spend on their wedding. Aja and José—like all couples—have four basic options when facing a decision about which both partners disagree and only one decision is possible (i.e., the couple cannot have a wedding that is both expensive and inexpensive at the same time): (a) Aja could agree to José's plan for the wedding, (b) José could agree to Aja's plan for the wedding, (c) the partners could seek a compromise that combines aspects of each partner's plans, and (d) the partners could disagree, not resolve the issue, and agree to end their relationship (or call off their wedding indefinitely). Note that there will be situations in which each of these options may be the best course of action. However, let's assume that this couple does not want to take the final option, and that they agree that each partner's concerns about the other partner's plans for the wedding have merit. This leaves them with the option of compromising to find a mutually agreeable decision.

To reach a compromise, the couple can ask themselves, "What is the ultimate goal we hope to achieve through this conversation?" Most likely, both Aja and José want to have a fun, special wedding in which all of their family members can take part. Working together with this goal in mind, the couple can compromise and reach a mutually satisfying decision. When compromising, it is often helpful for each partner to prioritize the aspects of the decision that are most and least important. Aja might say that her highest priority is that the couple will have some money left over after the wedding to begin to save for their house. José might decide that the most important aspect of this decision is to have all of their family members present at the wedding. Using this information, the couple can work toward planning a wedding that allows them to have all of their family members present but that is based on a reasonable budget that will leave them with an adequate amount of money after the wedding is over. When you and your partner reach similar decision points in your relationship, work toward a common goal through patient, understanding communication.

Case Study #3: Tanya and Ron

Ron prepared a nice, romantic dinner for Tanya a few weeks before their wedding. He spent a few hours preparing the meal and creating a relaxing environment with candles and flowers. Ron wanted to make this meal as a special treat for Tanya, because they both had been busy with their wedding plans and jobs during the past few months. They felt they hardly had any time to spend together lately, and it was beginning to take a toll on their relationship.

During the first few courses of the meal, Tanya remained pretty quiet. The couple was about to eat dessert when Tanya said, "I'm glad you finally made time for me in your busy schedule. It seems like you haven't cared too much about seeing me the past few weeks."

Ron felt attacked and hurt. After all, he made this nice dinner for Tanya, and they'd *both* been busy. He could not believe that Tanya would make such a comment when he had just gone to all of the effort to make a nice meal for her. Despite Ron's emotional reaction, he kept quiet and ate his dessert. He remained quiet for the rest of the night. When Tanya asked him what was wrong, he said, "Nothing." The evening ended with Tanya leaving Ron's house and both partners feeling hurt and confused about how such a potentially romantic evening could have turned out with the partners feeling even *more* disconnected than they felt before the meal.

What Can You Learn from This Example?

How did such a nice evening go so wrong? Ron and Tanya's evening provides a good example of how hurtful ineffective communication can be. Because you care so deeply about each other, you have the potential to hurt your partner—intentionally or unintentionally. Although it is unlikely that Tanya intended to hurt Ron's feelings, this conversation still left Ron feeling upset and disrespected. Tanya may have intended to make a caring remark (she probably really meant it when she said that she was glad that he made time for her), but her comment stung Ron nonetheless. Both Ron and Tanya could have changed their behavior that evening, which would have made for a much more pleasant meal.

Avoid Contemptuous Language

Whether or not Tanya intended for her comment to affect Ron the way it did, her comment came across as contemptuous and unappreciative. Tanya's statement, "It seems like you haven't cared too much about seeing me the past few weeks," implied that Ron was not making room for her in his life. That statement also implied that Tanya was concerned about him, even if he was not concerned about her. Consider an alternate statement that she could have used to express the sentiment that she was glad that they *did* have this time together: "I am so happy that we're spending time together. It means so much because of how busy we've been lately." Imagine what a different impact this statement would have had compared to Tanya's original statement! When a person makes a contemptuous statement, the recipient feels belittled and attacked. Contemptuous communication is one of the most damaging forms of communication within a marriage. The old adage to think before we speak holds especially true in marriage. Although it is not possible to anticipate every possible consequence of everything we say, choosing our words carefully can help to ensure that we use language that doesn't carry an attack on our partners.

Speak Assertively with "I Statements"

When Ron felt hurt by Tanya's statement, he accepted it passively. Ron decided not to share his feelings with Tanya, and he became quiet. During his silence, he continued to think negative thoughts. Ron's passive response to Tanya's comment prevented him from communicating honestly with her. One strategy Ron could have used to convey his reaction and remain respectful of Tanya would be to use an "I statement" to describe how he felt. In using I statements, we speak about our personal experiences, feelings, and responses. An I statement Ron could use is, "I felt hurt when you said that I haven't cared about seeing you lately." In this statement, Ron states clearly how he feels and the specific event that led him to feel that way. Compare that statement with the following aggressive response: "You were so rude when you said I didn't care about our relationship." In this "you statement," Ron judges Tanya, which will put her on the defensive. When communicating about your feelings and reactions, clearly describe your feelings and the behaviors that are associated with your response. I'll add one more caution about using I statements. Simply adding the words "I feel" to a hurtful statement does not automatically make it an I statement. For example, saying "I feel that you are an inconsiderate jerk!" is definitely not an effective way to communicate.

Demonstrate Concern and Respect for Your Partner's Feelings

Tanya could have been more inviting in asking Ron to share his feelings. Tanya probably recognized she had upset Ron—or at least she realized that something was wrong with him later in the meal. To help Ron feel more comfortable in talking with her, she would need to show him she really wants to hear what he has to say. For example, she might say, "I'm here for you, and I hope you will tell me if something I said upset you." Then she must listen actively to him!

In this situation, a romantic evening was ruined because of one remark. This turned into one messy dinner for Tanya and Ron! Incorrect assumptions, hurtful statements, and ineffective ways of expressing emotions took the place of a romantic ambience, a loving gesture of affection, and an opportunity for two partners to reconnect. You may have had similar experiences in your own relationship.

Case Study #4: Alexis and Nathan

Alexis comes over to the apartment of her fiancé, Nathan, after a long day at work. Alexis appears to be distracted, she has a very serious look on her face, and she demonstrates low energy when she greets Nathan. Nathan notices that Alexis appears to be upset, and he says to her, "It seems like you've had a rough day."

Alexis replies, "My boss gave me such a hard time today! I turned in that big project I've been working on, and he listed what seemed like a million things he thought were wrong with it. I worked so hard on that project. My boss couldn't even say one nice word about it."

Nathan knows that Alexis thinks this project would have been a big step for her career. He empathizes. "You worked so hard on that project. It must have been difficult to listen to your boss rip it to shreds."

Alexis nods, feeling that Nathan understands her. She says, "Yes, it was just awful."

Nathan goes on. "What else happened? What do you need from me right now?"

What Can You Learn from This Example?

Here's a case study that demonstrates great communication. You can learn just as much about communicating with your partner from examples of good communication as you can from communication mistakes. Nathan and Alexis both did many things well during this conversation. Work on emulating their conversation style in your own relationship.

Manage Intense Emotions Appropriately

First, Alexis is to be commended for talking about her problem with Nathan and not taking her anger out on him. She appears to have good insight into what is bothering her, and she is able to identify her emotional response to her frustrating situation at work. A temptation often exists to lash out at a partner when the anger is really directed at someone else. She resisted the option of picking a fight with Nathan as a way to release her anger built up from the day. Alexis avoided this temptation and shared her feelings openly with Nathan.

Notice Nonverbal Clues

Nathan used positive communication skills. From the moment Alexis entered the room, Nathan noticed her nonverbal signs of frustration and distress (including her energy level and her facial affect). One way to improve communication is to pay attention to your partner's nonverbal language. You can learn a lot by noticing how your partner looks or sounds while talking. Nonverbal language includes the expression on your partner's face, her posture, the rate and tone of your partner's speech, gestures she uses while speaking, and the degree to which your partner maintains eye contact with you. Every person uses unique forms of nonverbal communication to convey his or her emotions. Some nonverbal clues your partner might use to express his emotions include a rushed pace and tensed muscles (stress), fidgeting and blushing (nervousness), wide eyes and a loud voice (excitement), slumped posture and a long face (sadness), and a dazed look and lack of verbal communication (distraction). Nonverbal language is a powerful form of communication that is often more revealing than what your partner actually says. In fact, research has shown that less than 10 percent of communication is conveyed by the spoken word. The rest of the message is communicated by nonverbal signs. Pay attention to the messages your partner is sending to you via her nonverbal communication. You will develop a new understanding of your partner's inner experiences, which can help you to improve your verbal communication as well.

Validate Your Partner's Feelings

Next, Nathan let Alexis know that he was there to listen to her. He validated her feelings about her day, conveying to her that her feelings were normal and understandable given the circumstances. Validation goes a long way in fostering a strong connection between partners. When you send the message to your partner that "You're normal for feeling that way, and I understand," your partner feels heard and understood. Your partner also learns that she can share more information and emotion with you without being judged or dismissed. Remember, you do not have to agree with your partner to understand her feelings.

Convey Empathy Through Your Communication

Finally, Nathan used excellent communication skills when he used empathetic statements and validated Alexis's feelings.

Nathan's warmth, understanding, and empathy helped Alexis feel safe in sharing her feelings and experiences with him. Also, he helped her explore her reaction more deeply. Through continued conversations like this one, it is likely that Nathan and Alexis are on their way to a satisfying marriage. Apply the effective communication skills Nathan and Alexis used—managing intense emotions appropriately, noticing nonverbal language, validating one another's emotions, and conveying empathy and respect—to enhance the communication in your relationship.

Conclusion

Just as miscommunication is a source of stress in relationships, positive and adaptive communication skills can enhance your relationship. Communication skills provide the foundation for all the other topics addressed in this book. You won't be able to work on relationship issues if you can't communicate effectively with your partner about them! By maintaining open, supportive communication in your marriage, your relationship becomes stronger and more satisfying. Hopefully this section has shown you that you can replace ineffective communication strategies with more effective ones to produce more desirable patterns of communication. Your communication with your partner has the potential to cause great happiness or great distress—and all couples are likely to experience both extremes over time. Be careful when you communicate with your partner so your communication will enhance your relationship, not detract from it.

Research shows that couples that have positive communication early in their marriages are likely to demonstrate greater marital satisfaction later on. The couples in the case studies in this chapter experienced common communication situations. The strategies that I proposed to help these couples are the same strategies that can help you improve the communication within your relationship. Practice effective communication skills as often as you can, until they become second nature. Through mastering communication that conveys respect, understanding, and empathy, you and your partner will be able to strengthen all other areas of your relationship.

Action Plan: Communication Skills

1. Understand your and your partner's communication styles.

2. Aim for understanding.

3. Listen actively.

4. Be willing to compromise.

5. Avoid contemptuous language.

6. Speak assertively with "I statements."

7. Demonstrate concern and respect for your partner's feelings.

8. Manage intense emotions appropriately.

9. Notice nonverbal clues.

10. Validate your partner's feelings.

11. Convey empathy through your communication.

Discussion Questions

1. What do you do well when you communicate with your partner?

2. What is one thing you could do to improve the communication in your relationship?

3. How often do you feel that you understand your partner?

4. What are some situations in which it is difficult for you to communicate effectively?

5. What would you do if you felt that your partner was not understanding you while you were talking?

Ryan and Nicole have been married for two years. Ryan and Nicole, both age twenty-seven, hope to have three children. Both partners are very satisfied with their marriage, but they have hit an impasse. Ryan is ready to try to have a baby, but Nicole wants to wait a few more years. Ryan believes that the couple is financially and emotionally prepared for the demands of parenthood. However, Nicole doesn't believe that she has progressed to the point in her career where she would like to be prior to having children. She continues to take the birth control pills she has been using for the past two years, despite Ryan's requests for her to stop taking them.

Neither partner is willing to compromise on this issue. Every time they talk about it, a big fight erupts, and they both feel misunderstood. The couple has been at an emotional impasse over the past two months because of this issue—alternating between periods of tense silence and loud arguments. Ryan and Nicole are committed to the marriage but are unwilling to seek counseling. They believe that counseling is for "crazy" people, and they don't think that anyone could help them with this problem.

three
Attitudes and Beliefs about Marriage

Ryan and Nicole do not seek help from a professional counselor because they believe that "normal" people with "normal" problems do not seek counseling. They believe they can resolve this issue on their own, even though they have been unsuccessful thus far. Their beliefs about marriage, and what married people should do when they have problems, may prevent them from moving forward in their relationship. So far, both partners have been unwilling to examine and possibly modify their beliefs about counseling and the meaning of seeking help for their problems. They appear to prefer to hold on to this belief even if it costs them satisfaction with their current relationship. It seems that each partner is simply waiting until the other one caves in and changes his or her mind—representing another of this couple's beliefs about marriage that "time heals all wounds." Other beliefs come into play in this situation as well, particularly related to having children. Ryan seems to believe that certain relational milestones indicate that a couple is ready to become parents, while Nicole believes that she must accomplish certain career goals before she will be ready to have a child. All of these beliefs factor into this couple's decisions about how to respond to the current situation—and they are likely to influence the degree to which Nicole and Ryan are able to manage the stress related to this dilemma.

What do you believe about marriage? How similar are your and your partner's beliefs? How do these beliefs influence your relationship? How do your beliefs about other areas of your life—such as your career, families, and parenting—affect your relationship? In this chapter, we consider these questions and more. First, we explore how your current attitudes and beliefs toward marriage can influence your own marriage later on. You and your partner will complete an exercise to foster discussion about your beliefs about marriage. Then you will explore the origin of these beliefs and what you can do if your beliefs about marriage are not helping your relationship.

The Influence of Your Current Beliefs on Your Future Marriage

Your thoughts about marriage now, during your engagement, influence your marriage for years to come. Research shows that your premarital expectations about the happiness of your marriage can influence your ratings of marital satisfaction later on, and this is especially true for men. If you believe your marriage will be happy and satisfying, you are more likely to achieve this type of marriage. In contrast, if you expect your marriage to be unhappy, your marriage will probably not be satisfying. Your expectations relate to your partner, your relationship, and your role in the marriage. For example, your expectations might describe the type of spouse your partner will be, the amount of independence you will have in marriage, and the level of passion in your marriage. All of these expectations influence your actual experience within marriage.

Sometimes people place unrealistic expectations on themselves and their partners. For example, some people believe they should know exactly how to be a loving spouse before marrying. Other people believe that happily married couples *never* fight. Still others believe that certain people know "the secrets" to a great marriage—and that simply by learning these secrets and applying them to their relationships, they are guaranteed to live happily ever after. I know a lot about this latter belief from my experience being a marriage and family counselor who is married to another marriage and family counselor. More often than I could count, when people learn that my husband and I are both marriage counselors, they say, "Oh! You two must just have the best relationship!" I've begun to answer this reaction by saying, "That is a common misconception." The truth is, my husband and I struggle just like everyone else to maintain a positive relationship—and believe me, we have had some major fights in our relationship! We may have some unique skills and knowledge about relationships that we've gained through our professional training, but at the end of the day, we are just two people trying our best to build a strong marriage.

Unrealistic beliefs about marriage can cause problems over time. It is possible to hold extremely high expectations for marriage that you could never live up to in the real world. Although there may be some motivational aspects of aspiring to some ideal version of marriage, a more likely result is disappointment and frustration. Marriage is a learning process, and it is not possible to know how to act in every situation. In fact, the unexpected surprises that you will encounter over your years together will bring exciting opportunities for growth—both personal and relational. For most people, a marriage that is completely planned out from day one would be extremely boring! For all of these reasons, it is important for partners in a long-term, committed relationship to hold realistic but positive expectations for their marriage, with an open mind to changing those beliefs as new opportunities arise.

Your beliefs about marriage can either enhance your relationship or impede your efforts to create a satisfying marriage. As you prepare for marriage, it is important to take some time to reflect upon your beliefs about marriage and to decide which beliefs you want to continue to hold on to, and which beliefs you want to change. Complete the following exercise to explore the attitudes and beliefs that you and your partner have regarding marriage. Afterward, consider if you or your partner hold any other beliefs that were not included in the list.

Directions: Do you agree or disagree with the following statements? Write "Agree" or "Disagree" in the spaces provided. Ask your partner to do the same. Then compare your answers with your partner's answers. Discuss any differences between your beliefs.

PARTNER A	PARTNER B

▶ I believe a man should be the head of the household.

_____   _____

▶ I would feel comfortable going to marriage counseling if we couldn't resolve an issue on our own.

_____   _____

▶ I think it is a woman's responsibility to do the cooking, cleaning, and other household tasks.

_____   _____

▶ I can't think of any reasons that I would be willing to get divorced.

_____   _____

▶ I believe spouses should share the household responsibilities equally.

_____   _____

▶ I think spouses should maintain individual bank accounts, even if they combine most of their finances.

_____   _____

▶ I believe a marriage is not complete without children.

_____   _____

PARTNER A	PARTNER B

▶ I believe a marriage cannot be successful without passion and romance.

_____   _____

▶ I think most married people are happy with their relationships.

_____   _____

▶ My parents' relationship provided a good model of a successful marriage.

_____   _____

▶ I believe that married partners should spend most of their leisure time together.

_____   _____

▶ I think that happy couples communicate openly with one another about everything.

_____   _____

▶ I think that marriage is supposed to be fun.

_____   _____

▶ Couples that fight a lot should not stay together.

_____   _____

▶ In a marriage, it is important never to go to bed angry.

_____   _____

One way to understand how your current beliefs can influence your marriage is through the psychological concept of a self-fulfilling prophecy. A self-fulfilling prophecy is the idea that a person's expectation can lead to its own fulfillment. Your marriage can become a self-fulfilling prophecy because your beliefs about your partner and your marriage shape your experience. The following example provides an illustration of this concept.

When Steve was a child, his father frequently complained that wives are nags. Steve's father frequently made comments to Steve like the following: "See how your mom nags me all the time? All women are like that. They just never know when to leave a man alone." Now Steve believes his wife may become a nag as well. He acts in such a way that this becomes true. He puts off household tasks so his wife asks him repeatedly to do them. He also interprets her requests for assistance around the house as nagging. Steve's expectations become his reality. In his mind, his wife is a nag. Through his actions and thoughts, Steve created a situation that confirms his expectations about his wife.

You probably hold beliefs about your own future marriage. You probably also have expectations about what your partner will be like as your spouse. Many of these beliefs are probably positive, and they help you have a positive attitude toward your impending marriage. However, you may hold some beliefs or expectations that could prevent you from creating the type of marriage you desire. Once you identify your beliefs, you can change the less useful ones. One of the first steps in changing your beliefs is examining their origin.

The Source of Your Beliefs about Marriage

Whether your beliefs toward marriage are positive or negative, they were shaped by your life experiences and the world around you. You learn about marriage through the direct and indirect messages you receive from a variety of sources—such as family members, your peers, and the media. For example, watching romantic television programs (e.g., soap operas and romantic comedies) is related to idealized, romanticized beliefs about marriage and intimacy. The media exerts a powerful influence on societal attitudes about marriage.

When most people enter marriage, they have only had an "up close and personal" view of a small number of marriages, perhaps only one (i.e., their parents' marriage). Although you likely have known many married people throughout your life-time, your vision of most of these marriages is limited to the images that the couples project to the world. You can never really know what another person's marriage is like behind closed doors. Therefore, most people enter into marriage with gaps in their understanding of what marriage entails. People often turn to sources such as movies, television, and books in an attempt to fill in some of those gaps. People's imaginations often complete the rest of the pictures they hold in their minds about marriage. In my opinion, these dynamics contribute to the many unrealistic expectations and beliefs about marriage that many individuals hold. Marital expectations are often based on fantasies (from romantic movies or from one's one imagination) more than they are based on actual experience or evidence. It is no wonder, then, that the realities of marriage often fall short of spouses' original expectations.

By now, you have likely formulated a detailed conceptualization of your future marriage, based on your reactions to the lessons you've learned about marriage from your family, from the media, and from your peers. Some beliefs are more help-ful than others. Evaluate the messages that shaped your beliefs about marriage. Complete the following exercise to examine these messages.

Directions: The beliefs you hold about marriage result from the messages you receive from the world around you. Together with your partner, write the lessons you each learned about marriage from the following sources. Consider how each of these sources portrays marriage. At this point, do not make judgments about the usefulness of these beliefs. Simply consider what you learned about marriage from each source. Discuss your responses with your partner.

Example: A message you may have received from the movies: "Marriage should be between soul mates. When people are meant to be together, nothing can keep them apart."

What messages did each of the following sources send to you about marriage?

PARTNER A	PARTNER B
▶ The movies:	
_____	_____
▶ Television shows:	
_____	_____
▶ Your parents:	
_____	_____
▶ Your friends:	
_____	_____

PARTNER A	PARTNER B

▶ A religious institution:

_____   _____

▶ School/education:

_____   _____

▶ Books:

_____   _____

▶ The government:

_____   _____

▶ Other:

_____   _____

After completing this exercise, consider which sources of information were most influential on your personal attitudes toward marriage. Notice similarities and differences in the origins of your and your partner's beliefs. Discuss how the different sources of your beliefs influence your new marriage.

Strategies to Change Unhelpful Beliefs

Learning about building a solid marriage often involves a relearning process through which you will keep the lessons that you believe will help your marriage and get rid of or modify the lessons that are less likely benefit you and your upcoming marriage. Several strategies can help you modify unhelpful beliefs about marriage. The four strategies described in this section include: Developing awareness of your beliefs, examining the evidence for your beliefs, considering alternate interpretation, and seeking out more information about marriage.

Before you can change your beliefs, you need to become aware of those beliefs. People are often unaware of the beliefs they hold. The exercises in this chapter helped you identify your beliefs about marriage. Other ways to develop awareness of your thoughts about marriage include writing in a journal, keeping a list of your thoughts as you notice them, and talking about marriage with the significant people in your life. Simply taking time to reflect on your beliefs about marriage can help you identify the beliefs that are most influential on your expectations and behaviors within your relationship. Some of your beliefs about marriage may even come out through the wedding-planning process as you decide how to organize a wedding that reflects your relationship. For example, perhaps your desire to hold an outdoor wedding in an unconventional location reflects a desire to have less-traditional roles within your marriage. Or perhaps your plan to include children in your wedding ceremony indicates that you believe having children is an important part of a marriage. Pay attention to your and your partner's reactions and desires when making these types of plans, and see how it can add to your understanding of your beliefs about marriage.

Assessing Your Beliefs

Once you identify your beliefs, examine the evidence that supports or refutes them. For example, you may hold a belief that marriage counseling is only for couples that are thinking of divorce. To examine the evidence for this belief, you could interview a marriage counselor, read a book on marriage counseling, or ask couples that sought marriage counseling to tell you the types of things they discussed with their counselor. Through this research, you would discover that many couples enter counseling for reasons other than divorce. You will probably discover some evidence supporting and other evidence disproving your beliefs. Once you've gathered a great deal of evidence related to a specific belief you hold, you can evaluate whether the evidence indicates that your belief is reasonable. Gathering evidence about your beliefs helps you evaluate them objectively.

Consider other ways to interpret your beliefs. Your beliefs were shaped by your unique life experiences, so your views represent only one way of interpreting marriage. Consider your beliefs from other perspectives. For example, consider how a person of a different gender, ethnic background, or religious affiliation might have opinions that are different from yours. It may even be helpful to ask friends or family members with different perspectives to express their opinions about marriage. Viewing your beliefs from alternative perspectives helps you to examine the origins of your assumptions. Once you consider alternative viewpoints, determine which interpretation is most useful to you and your relationship.

Seek out information about marriage from couples that are already married. When I work with clients who seem to have unrealistic beliefs about other people's lives and relationships, I often encourage them to observe the world around them and pay attention to the many different types of people and relationships that exist. It is easy for most people to imagine that other people's lives are more interesting and their relationships are more loving than their own lives and relationships. Observe and interview married couples to learn about their experience of marriage. In doing this, you can learn more about the day-to-day experience of marriage. You are likely to be surprised to learn about what *really* goes on in other people's marriages. Although your marriage will not be identical to the couples you observe, you will learn about common sources of enjoyment, challenge, and stress for married couples.

Changing your beliefs, attitudes, and expectations about marriage takes time and effort. However, these changes are well worth the effort! Your marriage is more likely to thrive if you adopt accepting attitudes toward your partner and your relationship. Cognitive theories of psychology hold that changing your thinking patterns can lead to behavior changes. This suggests that any efforts you make to develop more positive, yet realistic, beliefs about marriage can help you to also adopt more adaptive behaviors within your relationships. Thus, developing positive attitudes about your relationship and partner supports the positive growth of your marriage.

Conclusion

Beliefs about marriage dramatically alter the course of a marriage. Many couples believe that marital unhappiness signals the end of their relationships and that it is not possible to regain lost happiness. Research demonstrates that this common belief is often untrue. In one study, 40 percent of people who gave the *lowest* possible rating of marital satisfaction at one point in time gave the *highest* possible rating of marital satisfaction just five years later. This is powerful evidence that marital satisfaction and beliefs about marriage can change dramatically over time. I also want to emphasize here that these dramatic changes can result from very minor shifts in a couple's relationship. Often, a small change can start off a powerful chain reaction that results in a seismic reorganization within a couple's relationship. For example, a couple who begins to use more positive communication skills—such as those discussed in Chapter 2—may find that all other areas of their relationship begin to improve as they learn to cooperate and convey respect for each other.

Most engaged people hold some positive and some negative expectations for their marriage. In this chapter, you learned how your current expectations influence your future marriage. You also examined the different sources of information that shaped your beliefs about marriage. Finally, you developed strategies to change the thoughts and expectations that could prevent you from attaining a satisfying marriage. Continue to work with your partner to develop the attitudes and beliefs that will help you to create a strong, satisfying marriage.

Action Plan: Attitudes and Beliefs about Marriage

1. Examine your beliefs about your future marriage.

2. Identify your unrealistic beliefs about marriage that could cause problems over time.

3. Examine the evidence for or against your beliefs.

4. Consider alternate interpretations of your beliefs.

Discussion Questions

1. What is one belief you hold toward marriage?

2. How could this belief influence your marriage?

3. What do you think are your partner's most influential beliefs about marriage?

4. What do you think are the biggest differences between your and your partner's beliefs about marriage?

5. What source shaped what you know about marriage?

Maria and Anthony will marry in six months. They meet weekly with the minister at their church for premarital counseling sessions. During a recent session, they talked about how they resolve conflict in their relationship. The couple said that they'd had very few "big fights" throughout their two-year courtship. Anthony said, "For the most part, we just get along really well."

During this conversation in premarital counseling, the couple realized that they have different styles of managing conflict. Maria likes to resolve conflict right away so they can get over it and move on. Anthony prefers to mull things over in his head first, and then talk to Maria after he calms down and thinks things through. Anthony doesn't like to argue when he's angry, because he might say things he would regret later. In the past, the couple has generally dealt with disagreements immediately, which Anthony says he's been able to manage because, "It's never really been anything big."

Maria and Anthony wonder what will happen when they face a major argument, which they both acknowledge is likely to happen at some point during their marriage. How will their different conflict management styles influence their ability to resolve such a conflict?

four

Conflict Resolution

Fortunately for Maria and Anthony, you can resolve conflicts even when you and your partner have different styles of doing so. Conflict is inevitable in marital relationships. Marriage is a union of two separate people with unique ideas and opinions. Spouses are certain to disagree about many of the issues they face, from minor preferences—like what to have for dinner—to larger preferences—such as when to have children or whether to move across the country. With the multitude of decisions that any given person needs to make on a daily basis, it is in many ways a wonder that couples actually ever agree enough to build relationships! You probably chose your partner over other prospective mates because you and your partner agree on a number of key issues. However, every couple experiences differences of opinion from time to time. This is a natural by-product of each partner building a strong sense of self within the relationship.

Conflict actually helps your relationship grow stronger, assuming you manage it well. For this reason, many premarital counseling programs help couples learn skills and strategies that help them manage conflict, and conflict resolution is one of the topics that the premarital counseling providers I surveyed rated as most important.

I will never forget the first fight my husband and I had after we married. It wasn't long before our first conflict arose. We were on the plane coming home from Costa Rica after our wedding and honeymoon. As so often happens, I do not remember the cause of our argument. However, I remember very clearly the feeling I had in my stomach while we were fighting. I thought, "What have I gotten myself into? This thing is headed for divorce. Maybe we can even stop the paperwork before the marriage is official!" I felt sick to my stomach as my thoughts continued to race, "We *have* to work this out. We have no choice. What if we can't work it out? I can't live like this!" Suddenly, the reality of the commitment I had just made came crashing down on me.

During our disagreements before we married, I could reassure myself that I could end the relationship if we could not work out our differences. After we married, we had no choice but to resolve our conflicts at whatever cost. I am happy to say that my husband and I resolved that first conflict somehow, as well as many others since then. You, too, may experience conflict in a new way after you get married. It is normal to feel differently about conflict once you make such a big commitment to your partner.

Many couples are surprised to learn that conflict helps enhance your relationship. Disagreements with your partner help you learn about your partner and how to establish boundaries for your relationship. In addition, you develop a more intimate connection with your partner as you resolve differences and reach a common understanding of the major issues you face. This chapter helps you examine how well you manage conflict in your relationship. You will learn skills for managing conflict effectively. You will also discover the different meaning of conflict within the context of marriage.

Conflict Management Styles

The manner in which you and your partner manage conflict says a lot about the quality of your relationship. This is not to say, however, that there is a *right* way and a *wrong* way to manage conflict. Every person has a unique approach to managing conflict. Couples manage conflict in different ways, and many different styles can lead to positive outcomes. There are, of course, certain types of conflict management that are maladaptive (that is, using violent behaviors to manage conflict is never an acceptable form of managing conflict—not to mention that violence in intimate relationships is illegal). Within reasonable limits, however, many strategies for managing conflict can work to help couples deal with their own issues, assuming that each partner agrees that that particular strategy is helpful. Complete the following exercise to consider how you and your partner manage conflict.

Directions: In the column below, each partner should circle the words that reflect how you feel and/or act during conflict. Compare your responses with your partner's responses to determine the similarities and differences between your conflict management styles. Once you circle all words describing your conflict style, put an "X" through any of the words that you would like to change.

PARTNER A	PARTNER B
☐ Peaceful	☐ Peaceful
☐ Loud	☐ Loud
☐ Volatile	☐ Volatile
☐ Respectful	☐ Respectful
☐ Calm	☐ Calm
☐ Angry	☐ Angry
☐ Violent	☐ Violent
☐ Avoidant	☐ Avoidant
☐ Aggressive	☐ Aggressive
☐ Quiet	☐ Quiet
☐ Regretful	☐ Regretful
☐ Hurtful	☐ Hurtful
☐ Nonchalant	☐ Nonchalant
☐ Attentive	☐ Attentive
☐ Embarrassing	☐ Embarrassing
☐ Nervous	☐ Nervous
☐ Sad	☐ Sad
☐ Patient	☐ Patient
☐ Scared	☐ Scared
☐ Frustrated	☐ Frustrated
☐ Lonely	☐ Lonely

Couples manage conflict using at least three different styles. John Gottman, a researcher at the University of Washington, identified the following three types of conflict management styles:

Volatile

Validating

Conflict-avoidant

During conflict, *volatile* couples are very expressive of their emotions. Partners in volatile relationships value independence and experience intensely the good and bad times in their relationships.

Validating couples typically have a friendly relationship. They approach conflict willingly when an issue is important, and they are moderately expressive of their emotions.

Conflict-avoidant couples agree to disagree about their differences, and they prefer to avoid high-intensity conflict.

Gottman's research indicates that when both partners in a relationship use the same style, a couple can manage conflict successfully most of the time. Problems arise when partners are unequally matched in their conflict management styles. For example, a relationship involving a person who prefers a volatile conflict management style and a person who prefers a conflict-avoidant style is likely to be characterized by a great deal of frustration, anxiety, and disagreement by both partners.

Now that you understand the differences between these conflict management styles, return to the previous exercise and compare your responses with your partner. If you notice major differences, be especially careful when conflict arises. It would be wise for you to have a conversation with your partner about your differing styles *before* you get into your next disagreement. Be respectful of your partner's unique style, and also be respectful of your own style. Then, figure out how you can combine your two styles into a new, unique style that fits for both of you. If your differing styles prevent you from resolving conflict, seek help from a professional counselor who can help you develop a conflict resolution style that works for both of you.

Conflict Resolution Skills and Strategies

You can use many skills and strategies to manage conflict in your marriage effectively. Conflict resolution skills are essential to managing the differences between you and your partner. As I stated earlier, conflict is an inevitable part of close relationships. Therefore, it becomes extremely important for you to develop strategies for managing conflict as it arises, in order to prevent it from taking over your relationship. Use the following nine strategies to enhance your ability to manage marital conflict.

Remain Calm and Self-Focused

When you face conflict, remain calm so that you maintain control over your behavior. Monitor yourself throughout the conflict, and be aware of signs that you are unable to participate productively in the conversation. These signs include an inability to listen to what your partner is saying, acting defensively toward your partner, and experiencing intense physiological symptoms of anxiety, such as a pounding heart rate, sweating, or a headache. If you feel overwhelmed, ask for a time-out so you can calm down. Begin calming down by taking some deep breaths and reminding yourself to stay calm. Once you've calmed down, try to slow the pace of the conversation so that you can continue to monitor your level of anxiety and discomfort within the conversation. In any conflict, focus on yourself as the primary agent of change. Ask yourself, "What am I doing to create or maintain this conflict?" and "What can I change about myself to bring about a positive resolution?" Acknowledge your responsibility and your power to create positive change.

Establish Ground Rules for Fighting

Develop ground rules to follow when you disagree. Discuss the types of comments or behaviors that are unacceptable during conflict. Also, discuss how to act toward one another when you fight. Examples of ground rules include the following: no name-calling, no screaming, no physical violence or threats, and listen carefully to each other during arguments. Once you establish ground rules, monitor yourself and your partner to ensure that you adhere to your rules. If one of you does not follow the rules, take a break and resume your conversation later. Use the following strategies as a basis for additional ground rules for managing conflict in your marriage.

When You Disagree, Focus Only on the Current Issue

Any time you are in conflict with your partner, ask yourself, "What is my goal for this conversation?" and "Do I want this fight to end?" If your goal is to come to resolution, you must remain focused on the issue at hand. Deal with one issue at a time, and resolve each issue separately. When couples bring up several issues during one disagreement, they quickly become overwhelmed, and the argument spirals out of control. Times of conflict are not the best time to bring up the past. Although the current disagreement might relate to past experiences, remain focused on the current issue. When couples raise many issues at once, they do what is known as *kitchen sinking*. When you bring up everything, including the kitchen sink, during your argument, you confuse the current issue, overwhelm your partner, and decrease the chances that you will resolve your disagreement successfully. Remain focused on a single, current issue to foster successful conflict resolution.

Avoid Destructive Communication Patterns During Conflict

Heated moments of conflict often lead people to say hurtful things to their partners. Such a comment cannot be taken back, and the sting from the comment endures after the fight is resolved. Negative comments toward your partner do not help anything. They do not resolve the conflict, they do not strengthen your side of the argument, and they do not help your partner feel any better about you. They will, however, tear you apart individually and as a couple.

Four types of negative communication patterns are particularly damaging to relationships. John Gottman ominously named these the Four Horsemen of the Apocalypse. These patterns include:

1. Criticism: berating your partner and disparaging her worth

2. Defensiveness: perceiving everything your partner says as an attack

3. Contempt: using statements or behaviors that belittle your partner and are intended to elevate you to a higher position

4. Stonewalling: withdrawing physically or emotionally from the argument

These communication patterns damage your conversation and your relationship. Monitor yourself during conflict to ensure that you do not engage in these behaviors. If you do engage in these behaviors, have the courage to acknowledge your error, and offer a sincere apology. Then, recommit to using more adaptive communication strategies through the remainder of the conversation.

Use Positive Communication Skills

Just as negative communication patterns during conflict are harmful, positive communication skills enhance your ability to resolve disagreements. Positive premarital communication is associated with the degree of satisfaction within later marital relationships, and effective communication is most important during conflict. Review the communication strategies that I described in Chapter 2. The same strategies that help you communicate effectively can help you resolve conflict.

Perhaps the most important communication skill to use during conflict is listening. During conflict, people tend to be more concerned with convincing their partners they are right than they are with listening to their partner. If you and your partner go back and forth without listening, you will never move closer to resolving your disagreement. Rather, you each become further solidified in your position, making it increasingly more difficult to ever reach a resolution. Listen to one another during conflict, wait patiently for your turn to speak, and establish a goal to understand each other throughout the conversation.

Never Allow Any Form of Abuse in Your Conflict

Abuse takes many forms, such as physical violence or intimidation, verbal aggression, or emotional attacks. Abuse between spouses is frighteningly common. Statistics suggest that about 16 percent of couples have experienced violence in their relationships. Violence occurs in marriages across social classes, ethnic and religious groups, and geographic areas, and both men and women can be victims of relationship abuse. *Any instance of abuse or violence in your relationship is cause to seek immediate professional assistance.* A single instance of intimidation causes serious harm, as it chips away your trust and respect in your partner. Your relationship cannot provide safety or security if you feel threatened by your partner or if your partner feels threatened by you. Relationships that are built upon the control and intimidation of one partner by the other are not healthy for either person. Your relationship should be a safe place for both you and your partner. Again, *never* allow any form of violence in your relationship.

Seek Professional Help When Necessary

Sometimes, it is difficult for couples to resolve conflicts on their own. Even after you use all of the conflict management strategies in this chapter, you and your partner may still be unable to resolve a particular issue. Although they are relatively uncommon, there are issues that can arise in marriage for which there can be no compromise. For example, a couple either has children or they do not—it is not possible for a couple to have part of a child, or to have a child part-time (not including such arrangements as becoming foster parents or sharing joint custody with a former partner). Unresolved conflicts cause great stress in a relationship, and you and your partner may not imagine any way to resolve such disagreements.

Fortunately, there are places where you can turn for help. Identify resources you could use before you need them. I think it's a good idea for couples to build up a "warehouse" of resources in the early stages of their relationships. Begin now to stockpile supportive relationships, positive relationship skills, information sources, and personal characteristics that you can draw upon at a later point in time. An additional source of relationship support comes from community professionals. Professionals are trained to help people resolve problems in their relationships, and they provide guidance and insight that you might not receive elsewhere. Many professionals have the training and experience that qualify them to help you through a difficult conflict. You may be able to return to the same person who provided you with premarital counseling, as you will know and trust that person. Find someone who both you and your partner trust. Ask the person to describe her qualifications related to working with couples. You can seek out counseling at any stage in your relationship. You do not need to wait until you and your partner reach a crisis in your marriage. Relationship counseling helps you resolve problems, and it can also enhance and strengthen your relationship.

Develop Strategies to Manage Unsolvable Issues

Most couples face some issues that they will never be able to resolve completely. For example, my husband and I have had a constant disagreement about romance; I want him to be more romantic, and he says that is just not the way he is. Because we have such different perspectives, we will probably never fully resolve this issue—although we have become less distressed by this issue over time. When you face such an issue, aim to come to a mutual agreement about how to manage it. At some point, you and your spouse will have to accept that you do not agree.

Accepting your partner's different opinions does not mean this issue won't rear its ugly head from time to time. Plan ahead how to manage the issue when it arises. For example, you could take turns getting your way, or you may decide to seek counseling when you reach another roadblock. Remember, it is normal and understandable for you and your partner not to agree on every issue. Respect each other, and seek alternative ways to live with your differences.

Try to Learn and Grow from Every Fight

Each conflict presents an opportunity for your relationship to grow stronger. Think about your disagreements and arguments as *growing pains*. Conflicts are part of the process through which you and your partner must go in order to develop a more intimate connection. Without conflict, your relationship may remain stagnant—perhaps even boring. Each resolved conflict represents an important accomplishment for your relationship. By resolving conflict, you demonstrate your ability to compromise and cooperate. When you experience the growing pains that result from conflict in your relationship, remember that they are usually temporary, and they are often a sign that something new and exciting is developing in your relationship.

Learn about yourself, your partner, and your relationship through every disagreement. After you resolve each conflict successfully, discuss the following question with your partner: "What can we learn from this disagreement?" There are many lessons to learn from fighting. For example, you may learn that you have different preferences for the type of lifestyle you want to live, you may learn that you communicate effectively during times of stress, or you may learn that your partner is willing to make sacrifices to make you happy. Then use these lessons to improve your conflict management strategies the next time a disagreement arises. Your relationship becomes stronger as you apply these lessons to help you create a mutually satisfying marriage.

Using the strategies described here when you face conflict will help you develop peaceful resolutions to disagreements. Conflicts are sources of stress for married couples. When couples use ineffective conflict resolution strategies, conflicts become hurtful, damaging, and more significant over time. As you and your partner practice the skills described in this chapter, the opposite will probably happen—your disagreements will provide opportunities for growth and deeper intimacy.

Conclusion

Conflicts and fights may take on a different meaning for you once you are married than they had while you were dating. When you marry, you make a commitment to spend the rest of your life with your spouse. Therefore, you may feel added pressure to resolve your fights peacefully. Especially in the early years of marriage, conflicts can give rise to additional fears and concerns about the overall state of the relationship. While you were dating, it was easier to break off the relationship if it was impossible to resolve a conflict with your partner. Conflict certainly takes on different meanings during the various stages of your relationship.

As you embark on your new marriage, consider how to improve your conflict management skills to produce better outcomes once you are married. The Action Plan below reviews the key conflict management strategies described in this chapter. Build on your existing strengths in managing conflict to further enhance your relationship. Practice the skills described in this chapter with your partner on a regular basis so you will be comfortable with them when you face major conflicts in your marriage. Conflict is a normal part of any relationship. Your marriage will grow as you resolve conflicts and work together to create a mutually satisfying relationship.

Action Plan: Keys for Conflict Management

1. Understand conflict management styles.

2. Remain calm and self-focused.

3. Establish ground rules for fighting.

4. When you disagree, focus only on the current issue.

5. Avoid destructive communication patterns.

6. Use positive communication skills.

7. Never allow physical, emotional, or verbal abuse to become part of your conflict.

8. Seek professional help when necessary.

9. Develop strategies to manage unsolvable issues.

10. Try to learn and grow from every fight.

Discussion Questions

1. When you think about the arguments you have had with your partner, how well do you think you came together to find a solution?

2. What could you do to resolve conflicts more smoothly?

3. What were your parents' conflicts like?

4. Do you prefer to resolve your conflicts immediately, or do you prefer to cool down first? Why?

5. What could you do if you and your spouse were not able to resolve a conflict on your own?

Alex feels that he never has enough time to do all the things he wants to do. He recently became engaged, and he feels terrible because he can't find more time to spend with his fiancée to work on their wedding plans. He feels guilty for making her do most of the work on their wedding, but he hasn't been able to rearrange his schedule to make more time.

Alex's job as a consultant requires him to spend a lot of time out of town, and he works long hours even when he is in town. Over the past several months, he has been working on a number of major projects that require a high level of energy and focus. In addition, Alex spends time helping his mother, who is undergoing treatment for breast cancer. She needs help around the house because she lives alone, and Alex wants to help any way he can.

Now, with the wedding plans, he's not sure how to fit everything in. He just wishes he could spend more time with his fiancée, which seems impossible given his busy schedule. Alex feels overwhelmed and exhausted when he thinks about how busy he is. At times, he convinces himself that this level of busyness is temporary, but he often wonders how much all of these time demands will continue once he is married.

five

Making Time for Your Relationship

Time does not stand still when you are engaged. Generally, you can't put everything else in your life on hold until the wedding is over. I hope you have more spare time than Alex, but his situation is common. You and your partner probably have many demands on your time, and those demands will continue once you are married. When life is busy, it is easy to take your partner for granted. You may expect your partner to be there for you once your schedule becomes less packed, so you put spending time together on hold. However, this is not the best strategy for managing time in your relationship. Neglecting your partner creates stress on your relationship, as your partner may feel that you do not care about him. When you do not create time for your partner, you will not be able to address important issues in your relationship—such as planning your future or resolving conflict.

While I was preparing for my marriage, my schedule was busier than ever. I was a graduate student, taking a course load of seventeen semester credit hours, completing a twenty-hour per week internship at a community counseling agency, teaching an undergraduate course with fifty-five students, *and* volunteering as a Girl Scout Troop leader (not to mention planning our destination wedding in Costa Rica). Just thinking back on that time makes me tired! I remember keenly the strain these time demands placed on my mental well-being and on our relationship. I hope that what I've learned since then can help you manage your time now better than I did then.

The premarital counseling providers I surveyed rated "the importance of spending time with one's partner" as the fifth most important topic to address with premarital couples. Although it makes sense that couples would need to spend time together in order to work on the other topics in this book, the topic of time management is not typically the first thing that comes to mind when thinking about preparing for marriage. However, time spent with your partner allows you to become stronger in all other areas of your relationship—assuming you use that time wisely. This chapter helps you address time-related issues. First I discuss how society works against your best efforts to create time for your partner. Then I ask you to describe your time orientation and the compatibility of your and your partner's time orientations. Finally, you will learn time management strategies to help you carve out time from your busy schedule to devote to your partner.

A Busy Society

In modern society, people face many demands on their time. People today work longer hours and take shorter vacations than ever before. Cultural norms define people by achievements, so many people feel pressure to use every moment of their day to work toward accomplishing more tasks. These cultural norms place major demands on marital relationships. Even today when many people are aware of the importance of maintaining balance across different areas of life, a lot of companies still place a higher value on career accomplishments than they do on supporting their employee's family lives. In this way, modern society is not conducive to successful marriages, which take time and energy to maintain.

Married people face many demands on their time—such as careers, community involvement, physical health, leisure activities, friendships, and other areas of life. Individuals work long hours at their jobs, and many jobs today require a high level of skill and intellectual engagement. By the time they return home to their families, workers are tired, frazzled, and stressed out. With many commitments competing for your time, you may feel you do not have time to devote to your relationship. It is all too easy to come home after a busy day of work and space out in front of the television rather than spending time in meaningful contact with your partner.

During the first few years of marriage, you may experience other major transitions—such as starting a new career, changing jobs, moving to a new location, having children, and becoming involved in your community. All of these changes bring positive opportunities your way, yet they can place extraordinary demands on the time and resources you have available to devote to your partner. You can expect that your life will probably become busier in the coming years—unless you work actively to develop a balanced time management strategy. Spending time with your partner is essential now and in the years to come, and this time should be an essential component of any time management strategy you develop. This chapter will help you develop strategies for creating the time that your relationship requires to survive and flourish.

What Is Your Time Orientation?

Based on your cultural background and life experiences, you develop a distinct orientation toward the manner in which you perceive time. Understand your time orientation by considering whether you are oriented toward *being* or *doing*. The following exercise will help you examine your and your partner's time orientations. Then, read on to learn how you can use this information to enhance your relationship.

Directions: Indicate whether each statement is mostly true or false for you. Ask your partner to do the same. Score your responses according to the following directions.

PARTNER A	PARTNER B

▶ 1. I like to be busy.

True _____   False _____   True _____   False _____

▶ 2. The most important goal I have for my life is to be a good person.

True _____   False _____   True _____   False _____

▶ 3. It is difficult for me to relax.

True _____   False _____   True _____   False _____

▶ 4. I feel constricted by a structured schedule.

True _____   False _____   True _____   False _____

▶ 5. I feel anxious when I have nothing to do with my time.

True _____   False _____   True _____   False _____

▶ 6. I would describe myself as a laid-back, spontaneous person who likes to go with the flow of life.

True _____   False _____   True _____   False _____

▶ 7. I usually set goals for how much I'd like to accomplish each day.

True _____   False _____   True _____   False _____

▶ 8. I am happiest when I have free, unstructured time.

True _____   False _____   True _____   False _____

▶ 9. The most important goal I have for my life is to accomplish something significant.

True _____   False _____   True _____   False _____

▶ 10. I find it very easy to unwind.

True _____   False _____   True _____   False _____

Scoring Directions: You have two sets of scores. First, add the number of "True" responses for the odd-numbered questions (1, 3, 5, 7, 9). This is your *Doing* score. Next, add the number of "True" responses for the even-numbered questions (2, 4, 6, 8, 10). This is your *Being* score. Compare your Doing score with your Being score. The higher score represents your time-orientation. If your scores are even, you are oriented equally toward being and doing. Compare your scores with your partner, and notice the similarities and differences in your responses.

What did you discover about your time orientation from this exercise? If you are oriented toward being, then you probably are more spontaneous and flexible in scheduling your time. You define yourself by who you are rather than what you do, and you enjoy unstructured, free time. If you are oriented toward doing, then you probably enjoy a structured schedule. Your self-concept is based on your accomplishments, and you use time management to increase your achievements. Neither of these time orientations is better than the other—and each has its own unique advantages. However, your orientation toward time influences your life and relationships.

Consider the differences and similarities between you and your partner regarding your time orientations. My marriage provides an example of a relationship between partners with different time orientations. I am a "do-er," and my husband is a "be-er." This dynamic has been extremely influential on our relationship and the manner in which we spend our time together. I like to be busy and active, so I often want to find something fun and active to do together. My husband prefers to relax, and he is content to just sit and do nothing together. Vacations and weekends are often challenging for us, as we struggle to balance my need for activity and his need for rest and quiet. Although our time orientation differences present challenges, we also complement each other well. I like having him around to remind me to relax. Likewise, my husband appreciates that I encourage him to try new experiences. Think about your own relationship and the differences and similarities in your time orientations, as well as how you can use this information to understand how you and your partner manage time in your relationship.

Strategies to Find Time for Your Relationship

You may feel that you never have enough time to get everything done that you would like to accomplish. You are probably right. There is always something else you could be doing with your time that could help you to make progress toward achieving goals in many areas of your life. For example, you *could* be exercising more, spending more time with family and friends, working more on a job- or school-related project, volunteering in the community, and the list goes on. . . . Effective time management requires you to be clear about your priorities and devote the most time and energy to the most important areas of your life. In this section, I present time management strategies to help you create time for your relationship.

Set Goals for Your Relationship

When you have goals for your life and relationship, you are able to prioritize how you spend your time. If you and your partner share a goal of creating a loving relationship, you easily make decisions that help you reach that goal. Make specific goals about how much time you want to spend together. For example, you may set a goal for you and your partner to spend at least two evenings each week together. I find that it's often helpful for couples to schedule time with each other in order to reserve that time as "couple time." (Some people might argue that this strategy can hamper spontaneity within a relationship. However, scheduled time does not have to replace the spontaneous activities within your relationship. It just helps to guarantee that you will have at least some time available for your relationship.) Then chart your progress toward your goals. Notice if, over time, you see a pattern of canceling your regularly scheduled dates for the sake of working longer hours or some other commitment. If so, you may need to reschedule your dates for another day or time, or you may need to work on developing more clear boundaries between your relationship and the other areas of your life. Together with your partner, structure your time in accordance with your goals.

Maintain Balance in Different Areas of Your Life

When your marriage is a top priority, you can decide which other areas of your life are less important and demand less time and attention. Prioritizing the different areas of your life may also involve cutting down the time you spend on activities that are not directly related to the most important areas. Maintaining balance across the different parts of your life does not mean that every area of your life receives the same amount of time. Early in relationships, some couples devote all of their time to each other and neglect other areas of their lives—such as friends, family members, or careers. Do not allow this to happen to you; if you do, you may wake up one day to realize that you are isolated within your relationship. Maintain separate interests and activities outside your relationship so you can enjoy experiences with and without each other. Maintaining balance in the different areas of your life involves making time for your partner and the other important areas of your life.

Learn to Say "No"

You make the ultimate decisions about how you spend your time. Other people often seem to control our time—such as when other people ask for favors or we feel obligated to go to events we do not want to attend. It is difficult to say "no" when other people ask for our help or time. As you take control over your decisions about how you spend your time, you will find that you cannot fulfill every person's requests of you. Decide which activities are most important to you and which activities you are not interested in doing. Practice saying "no," and prepare to stand your ground. Ultimately, it is not in your best interest or the best interest of the person requesting the favor of you if you complete the task begrudgingly. Although it is difficult to say "no" at first, you will benefit ultimately from greater clarity about your needs and from having extra time to spend on the activities you enjoy.

Allow for Spontaneity in Your Schedule

Allow some time to be unstructured so you have free time with your partner. When every moment of your day is scheduled, you become overwhelmed by your obligations. Even time spent with your partner can seem like an obligation if it is scheduled tightly into your day. Many of the special moments you and your future spouse have shared probably were unplanned. In your future life together, you can continue to share many fun, spontaneous times with each other—even as the demands on your time increase. To allow these moments to happen, leave time in your schedules for just hanging out and enjoying each other's company. In my marriage, my husband and I typically reserve Saturdays as unplanned days. Sometimes, we end up going out and having fun in the community, and on other Saturdays we just stay home and hang out around the house. When we do go out and do something on those days, we're usually doing it because we really want to, and not just because it was in our schedule so we felt like we had to.

Know Where Your Time Goes

Many people who feel they never have enough hours in the day have no idea where their time goes. Most people go through their days without paying attention to the amount of time they spend on a given activity—or how that time adds up during a week. Before you make changes in the way you spend your time, know where your time goes. Spend a week recording what you do and how much time you spend on each activity. Ask your partner to do the same. You may discover, for example, that you spend an average of two hours watching television every day of the week, for a total of fourteen hours of TV time each week (equaling almost one full day's worth of waking hours!). It's up to you to decide whether that is a constructive, meaningful use of your time. However, you may discover that you could use your time more constructively by spending some of that time on your relationship or your work-related tasks. Once you both know how you spend your time, discuss the changes you each want to make. Create a new schedule that takes into account the unique demands of your individual time requirements and your desires to spend time together.

Practice Mindfulness

It is possible to be with your partner, but to not *really* be with your partner. In other words, you are in the presence of your partner, but your mind is elsewhere—perhaps on that big presentation you're giving tomorrow, or your mother's upcoming birthday party, or your plans for volunteering in the community next week. Mindfulness is paying attention to the present moment. When you have time with your partner, make the most of it. Notice all of the wonderful things about him. Focus your senses entirely on your partner—the smell of his cologne, the look of the smile on his face, the sound of your partner's voice, or the touch of the massage your partner is giving you. Push aside your thoughts of what you need to do later. Forget about the things going on around you and enjoy simply being with your partner. Becoming more mindful often takes time, and many people find that it is much more difficult than it sounds. So, practice focusing on each other to make your time together meaningful.

Enjoy Your Time in Premarital Counseling

Many couples find the most valuable aspect of premarital counseling to be the opportunity to spend time with one another. If you go through premarital counseling, it will be a special time for you to enjoy learning about each other. Although there's another person in the room—your counselor—you can still use your counseling sessions as valuable times for strengthening your relationship. Quality time shared between partners is a valuable component of satisfying relationships, and premarital counseling provides that opportunity. Premarital counseling offers you and your partner the time and freedom to talk openly without distractions. If you go to premarital counseling, enjoy the opportunity to share this special time with your partner.

Conclusion

As you prepare to get married, your schedule may become more packed than ever. You are busy making plans for the wedding and your life after the wedding—on top of all of the regularly scheduled activities of your daily life. You will still have demands on your time once you are married and settled into your day-to-day routines. Make time together a priority, now and in the future. As you commit to creating time for each other, you demonstrate appreciation for your partner and your relationship.

Action Plan: Making Time for Your Relationship

1. Understand your and your partner's time orientation.

2. Enjoy your time in premarital counseling as special time with your partner.

3. Practice mindfulness when you are with your partner.

4. Know where your time goes.

5. Allow for spontaneity in your schedule.

6. Learn to say "no."

7. Maintain balance in the different areas of your life.

8. Set goals for your relationship, and schedule your time to help you reach your goals.

Discussion Questions

1. What do you think will be the biggest demands on your time once you are married?

2. What is your favorite thing to do when you spend time with your partner?

3. What can you do during busy times to ensure that you have time for your partner?

4. What is your time orientation—toward being or doing? What about your partner? How compatible are your and your partner's approaches to managing time?

5. How well do you manage your time in general? How do your time management habits influence your relationship?

Aaron and Vanessa are four months away from their wedding. Vanessa has full custody of her five-year-old daughter, Katie, from a previous marriage. Aaron has no children, but he has always wanted to have a lot of children. Aaron gets along great with Vanessa's daughter, and the three of them are excited about the upcoming wedding.

During a premarital counseling session, their counselor asks the couple who will be responsible for disciplining Katie. Aaron replied, "Vanessa will," at the same time Vanessa says, "We both will."

Aaron goes on, "That is Vanessa's job. She's good at it, and I don't think that Katie will listen to me. I'm just not comfortable disciplining Katie right now."

Vanessa responds, "But I won't be there all the time. Even though she's been living under my rules, we need to work together to create new rules to fit our new situation, and we'll have to share the responsibility of enforcing those rules."

Throughout the remainder of the session, the counselor works with the couple to develop a plan for how both partners will be involved in Katie's discipline in a manner that is comfortable for them and appropriate for Katie's needs.

six
Parenting and Children

The premarital counseling providers I surveyed indicated that the topics of parenting and children are very important for engaged couples to consider. Many engaged couples wish to discuss parenting issues before they marry. This conversation differs for each couple, based on their current situations and expectations for the future. Parenting issues that are often relevant for engaged couples include when to have children, who will be primarily responsible for the children's care and how parenting responsibilities will be shared, the number of children each partner hopes to have, and disciplinary issues for couples in which one or both partners already has children—just like Aaron and Vanessa in the previous case study. You and your partner may already have children. You may plan to have children soon, or you may wish to wait several years. You may have even decided that you do not ever want to have children. Whatever your situation, discuss your plans related to parenthood and children while you are engaged.

In this chapter, I address several issues related to parenting and children. First, I discuss the decision of when to have children, if at all. Next, I consider how becoming parents influences your marital relationship. Finally, I describe some special situations—such as getting married when one or both partners already have children and deciding not to have children.

Parenting Decisions

Couples face a number of important decisions related to parenting. Discuss these decisions as part of your preparations for marriage. One significant decision couples face is whether or not to have children at all. Some couples decide not to have children, and this may be a difficult, yet responsible, decision to make. The last section in this chapter discusses issues related to that decision. This section outlines important considerations for couples that decide to have children.

People have many reasons for wanting to become parents. You may want to have children because you love being around children, you believe you and your partner would make good parents, or you think that being a parent is an important task of adulthood. Whatever your reasons are for wanting to become parents, they will influence your decisions about when to have children. A number of other factors also play into couples' decisions about when to have children, notably financial and career-related issues. Although surprises can happen, and couples can become pregnant without much preplanning, modern birth control options allow couples to have a large degree of choice over the number of children they have and when they have children.

How will you and your partner decide on the right time to have children? There is no easy answer to this question. Couples do not usually wake up one morning and suddenly feel ready to have children; this is usually a gradual process that is influenced by many factors. Sometimes, partners disagree about when to begin to have children, which can create a great deal of stress and conflict in a relationship, which we saw in the case study of Nicole and Ryan in Chapter 3. You and your partner will probably spend a lot of time discussing your plans before you become parents. During these discussions, consider the following questions.

Do you both possess the personal resources required of parenting? A child requires a lot of time and energy. Until you both feel that you have the necessary resources to be a parent, having a child could pose a great risk to your relationship and the child. If you have a baby before one of you feels ready, your relationship could suffer from resentment, stress, and unmet expectations. When you both feel prepared, each of you are more likely to be supportive during this major life change.

If you or your partner does not feel ready to have children, how will you know when you are ready? Some people want to accomplish certain things before they have children (e.g., traveling, starting a business, or completing graduate school). For other people, the desire to have children does not come until the partners strengthen their marriage. Still other people are not ready until they feel mature enough to handle the increased responsibility. You and your partner may have different ideas about becoming ready to be a parent. Discuss how you can support each other as you progress toward feeling ready to become parents.

How will you and your spouse continue to care for your marriage once you are parents? Parents should not neglect their own relationship to focus exclusively on the child. When this happens, the marital bond weakens, leaving both partners feeling alone. Discuss strategies you can use to keep your marriage in focus after you have a child—such as planning regular dates alone with your partner, making time for sexual intimacy, and continuing to share discussions about other parts of your life with your partner. In the long run, maintaining focus on your marriage benefits you, your relationship with your spouse, and your children.

What will you do to manage marital conflict once you have children? Marital conflict can have a negative impact on children, although it is healthy for children to observe their parents managing conflict successfully. Of course, you and your spouse will continue to face conflicts once you have children, and in fact a new child brings with it a number of new potential issues to disagree about, such as who will get up at night when the baby is crying, who will make arrangements for day care, and how much money to save each month toward the child's future. Managing conflict becomes more important than ever because ineffective conflict management has a stressful impact on children. Before having children, conduct an honest self-evaluation of how well you manage conflict. This self-reflection helps ensure that you will provide a safe, nurturing environment for your child's growth. Develop strategies to manage conflict, especially during times of stress.

What can you and your partner do to become more prepared for the job of parenthood? Many couples lack formal or informal preparation in parenting skills. Fortunately, several resources are available for you and your partner to help you prepare to face the challenges involved in parenthood. Several excellent books and classes exist to help you learn parenting skills. Nothing can substitute actual time spent with children, however, which provides you with experiences that are similar to the demands of parenting. You and your partner may be able to baby-sit the children of a friend or family member. Also, find opportunities to volunteer together to work with children—such as in a church nursery, community organization, or local day care center. When you share these experiences, you learn more about working together to manage the stress of being around children. Finally, share other responsibilities to practice working together and negotiating your roles. For example, having a pet might provide you with practice in a pseudo-parenthood situation. Many couples have shared with me how much having a dog helps them learn to share responsibility when providing care for another living being.

What would you and your partner do if you experienced infertility in your relationship? Infertility causes stress in a marriage, as it challenges each partner's expectations and hopes for the relationship. Infertility, which affects 10 to 15 percent of couples that hope to have children, profoundly influences the relationships of couples that hope to conceive on their own. Couples face many decisions when confronted with infertility—such as whether to continue to try to conceive naturally, whether to adopt, and whether to undergo fertility treatments. Infertility treatments can be complicated and costly, which places great demands on a relationship. You cannot predict what will happen in your marriage as you attempt to conceive. However, it is wise to discuss with your partner how you might respond to infertility. This discussion helps you clarify your desires and prepares you for decisions you could face.

How do you think your relationship would be affected if you had a child with special needs? Although you cannot prepare for every possible unique challenge you may face as parents, it is helpful to discuss before you become parents how your relationship could be affected in the event that you have a child with special needs. Parenting a child with special needs can give rise to a number of unique challenges. These challenges will vary depending on the type of special needs the child has (for example, physical, cognitive, developmental, and/or behavioral needs). A discussion about the support you may need in order to best support a child with special needs can help you to identify resources that you can develop before you have children to strengthen your capacity for parenting—whether or not you do have a child with special needs.

All of the previous questions represent issues for you and your partner to address if you plan to have children. Building a strong marital relationship is the best way to prepare for the demands of parenthood. Whether you plan to have children soon after you marry or in the distant future, discussing these issues helps you join with your partner in planning your future family.

Children and Your Marriage

Couples' decisions about whether and when to have children are often influenced by their expectations of the effects children will have on the marriage. Couples that expect that having a child will help strengthen their relationship will most likely be more enthusiastic about having children than couples that expect that having children will in some way damage their intimacy. Becoming parents has a huge impact on a relationship. Although welcoming a new child into the family brings joy, it is also a stressful life event for you, your partner, and your relationship. This section describes some of the ways your marriage might change if and when you have children. Awareness of these issues helps you make parenting decisions once you are married.

Adjusting Your Roles

Having children requires you to adopt new roles within your relationship. Your roles as husband and wife change as you relate to each other as coparents in addition to your relationship as spouses. For example, a dual-career couple that values its egalitarian relationship may shift into new roles if one parent decides to stay home with the child while the other works. The spouse at home may shift into a homemaker role, while the other partner takes on the breadwinner role. With these new roles, each person is likely to take on different responsibilities within the family. Role changes require flexibility and adaptability in order to meet the new demands that arise with parenthood. With parenthood, your normal routines become complicated by the addition of a new person into the family.

Adjusting to Your New Family

The transition to parenthood brings many other adjustments and decisions. Caring for a child is a tremendous responsibility, and you and your partner will face exciting challenges as you learn to parent together. Many couples with a new child experience a change in their sexual relationship. Having a baby does not mean that you won't have sex for the next eighteen years until the child moves out of the house. However, you will need to work harder to create the time and energy for your sexual relationship. Other adjustments that new parents often face include a change in the family's financial situation, new social networks, and increased challenges related to traveling. Through all of these changes, it is important to continue to care for your marriage even as you care for your child.

Many couples also experience a change in one or both partners' careers when they become parents. Have you and your partner discussed what will happen in your careers once you have a child? Couples use many different arrangements to balance their jobs and families. Some family/career-related issues to consider include the following: each partner's career goals, whether one partner wants to stay home to raise the children, the flexibility of your job requirements, available resources for child care, and support you may receive from your social network, including friends and family members. If both of you continue to work full-time after becoming parents, you will encounter many other adjustments, such as different household responsibilities and accommodating your work demands to the baby's schedule.

Children can also influence the level of conflict in a marriage. Parenthood may reignite longstanding differences and give rise to new conflicts. In particular, having a baby can intensify arguments about household tasks. New parents typically feel overwhelmed by the demands of parenthood, and these feelings can lead to increased conflict and tension in the marriage. Therefore, couples should have strong problem-solving and conflict resolution skills as they transition to parenthood. Review the information in Chapters 4 and 10 for more information about conflict resolution and problem solving.

Not all of the changes associated with becoming parents are negative and stressful. Becoming parents can help you and your partner move to a new level of closeness as you share the experience of caring for a child together. The new experiences that parenthood brings can help your relationship grow stronger as you face these challenges together and enjoy fun moments with your child. Becoming parents heralds a new, exciting phase of life.

Getting Married with Children

Some couples face immediate parenting issues when they marry. If you and/or your partner are bringing children into your marriage, you will face unique challenges when you combine your families. The nature of these challenges will depend on custody and living arrangements, the amount of time that you and your partner have been a couple before marriage, the quality of the relationship between the children and the new stepparent, and the age of the children. Blended families often face complicated role adjustments. You will each redefine your roles in relation to your new spouse and the children. For example, you may make new arrangements regarding the discipline of the children and the family's daily schedule. Stepparents need to establish their roles as parents in the family, which may present conflict and frustration for the children and the parents. In addition, children may have a difficult time adjusting to having new people living in their home and taking away the undivided attention of their parent. Some children begin to display acting out behaviors around the time of their parent's new marriage.

Loyalty conflicts are common in blended families. Children often feel a sense of loyalty to their other biological parent, leading them to question the new stepparent's authority. The stepparent feels tension between desires for being liked by the children and having parental authority. All of these dynamics can lead to increased stress on the couple's new marriage. Before you marry, discuss strategies you will use to handle these arrangements. These strategies could include holding regular family meetings to discuss your progress, setting aside individual time for each parent to spend with his/her biological children, and developing clear arrangements about how disciplinary issues will be handled in the family—just like the counselor helped Aaron and Vanessa do in the case study at the start of this chapter. Involve your children in the discussion, as they play an important role in your adjustment to marriage. The characteristics that will help you have the most positive adjustment for you and the children include flexibility, patience, realistic expectations, and a strong marital relationship. Plan to face the unique challenges and exciting opportunities that will arise as you create your new family.

Deciding Not to Have Children

Over the past few decades, people in the United States have become more accepting of the choice not to have children. Couples decide not to have children for many reasons—such as a preference for enjoying life without children, a wish to focus their energy toward careers or other life pursuits, or a feeling that they are not cut out to be parents. People who decide not to have children usually make this difficult decision carefully. My personal belief is that it is commendable for couples that don't want to have children to remain childless. There are many ways to lead a satisfying, productive life.

Challenges of Childless Couples

If you and your partner do not want children, you may face some unique challenges in your relationship. First, you may face pressure or disappointment from people in your lives who expect you to have children. Your parents may be upset because you will not provide them with grandchildren. Explain the decision you have made, and be honest about your plans. It may seem easy to provide others with false hope that you may one day have a child, but this can ultimately lead to more pressure and dishonesty. You may even want to talk with these family members about other ways they could have opportunities for interacting with children, such as volunteering at an after-school program or becoming a mentor for a young child.

You might also struggle to define your relationships with other couples. At some point, your friends may all have children, which can lead to a shift in their preferences for social activities and topics of conversation. Consider how to maintain these friendships when your life experiences become different. You may benefit from focusing on other mutual interests, such as a hobby or related career experiences. Also, work on building new relationships with people with whom you feel supported in your decision to remain childless.

Perhaps the greatest challenge you could face is if one partner later changes her mind and wishes to have children. This is an extremely divisive issue for couples because compromise is impossible. You either have children or you do not; there is no middle ground. No easy solutions exist. Discuss now whether there are any situations in which either one of you could change your mind and how you could resolve this issue if it arises. If you and your partner confront this issue, you may wish to seek professional counseling.

Conclusion

Parenting and children are the source of much pleasure in a marriage, yet they also provide your relationship with unique, demanding tests of the strength of your bond. Although you cannot prepare for all of the dilemmas you will face related to parenting, you can consider now how you will make parenting decisions in the future. In addition, think about the hopes and expectations each of you holds in regard to parenthood. Be honest about these issues now, and work to create a common understanding of each partner's desires and concerns related to parenting.

Action Plan: Parenting and Children

1. As you prepare for marriage, talk with your partner about whether or not you wish to have children and how you will know you are ready for parenthood.

2. Learn more about the joys and demands of parenthood to develop realistic expectations about what is involved in raising children.

3. If you and/or your partner are bringing children into your marriage, talk openly with your partner to ease the transition to combining your families.

4. If you and your partner decide that you do not want to have children, prepare for how you can handle questions, concerns, and pressure to change your mind from other people in your life.

Discussion Questions

1. How many children do you want to have? What are your reasons for wanting to have that many children?

2. What kind of parent do you think you would be?

3. If you have decided that you do not want to have children, can you imagine any situations that might make you change your mind? If so, what are they?

4. If you have decided that you want to have children, how will you know that you are ready to become a parent? How will you know that your partner is ready?

5. What are some things that couples can do to keep their marriages a priority after becoming parents?

Toni and Sam married six months ago.

Prior to their wedding, they maintained a long-distance relationship for three years. During this time, they visited each other on weekends and spent time together over the holidays. They talked on the phone daily and maintained frequent contact through e-mail.

Because of the distance that separated them for so long, both Toni and Sam are excited that they now live together in the same city and house. Sam moved to live with Toni in a different state, and he is still trying to find a job in his new town.

Understandably, Toni and Sam are having a difficult time adjusting to their new life together. Because they lived so far apart, they had little time to learn about each other's "quirks," as they call them. For instance, Toni was surprised to learn that Sam spends thirty minutes in silent meditation every evening of the week. Likewise, Sam was surprised to learn that Toni leaves dirty dishes in the sink for a whole week before cleaning them.

These little surprises, as well as more significant differences in their lifestyles, led to a difficult adjustment period—although the couple reports that they are becoming more comfortable with these adjustments as time passes.

seven

Adjusting to Married Life

Whether you and your partner have lived together for years before getting married or have lived in separate states like Toni and Sam, your marriage vows bring many adjustments—big and small—to your life and relationship. You are facing a major life change that requires a period of adjustment as you adapt to life as a married couple. There is nothing inherently good or bad about change, but some people have more difficulty adjusting to change than others. People also respond differently to change at different stages of their lives. This chapter reviews the role that change plays as a couple adjusts to married life. Included in this chapter, you will find strategies to help you ease the adjustments of new marriage.

The Many Changes of Marriage

It is normal for couples to experience problems and conflict as they adjust to marriage. The most common areas of conflict for newlyweds are balancing job and family, the sexual relationship, finances, household responsibilities, and communication problems. I address these issues in more detail throughout this book; this chapter focuses on general change processes within couples' relationships. Any change within a couple's relationship has the potential to be a source of conflict as partners establish a shared life.

You and your spouse will have moments when transitions seem smooth and easy. During these moments, compromise seems simple, your partner seems understanding, and you feel proud of the strength of your love for one another. Hopefully, these moments are not overshadowed by the times when transitions are more complicated. In all likelihood, it will take time to adapt to the changes you face as you adjust to your new marriage. Becoming married signifies a big transition, even if you and your partner have already been living together for some time.

The legal contract that binds married couples is the primary difference between cohabiting couples and married couples. Regardless of how happy you are to get married, your marriage is a major life event that has the potential to bring you a lot of stress. Not all stress is bad. Some stress, called *eustress*, relates to positive events in a person's life. Chances are, you are willing to take some stress along with your wedding and your marriage, because you hope the ultimate result will be a lifetime of happiness with your partner. Just because an event is stressful does not mean you must avoid it at all costs. Some of the most rewarding parts of life—reaching a major accomplishment, having close relationships, and enjoying new opportunities—entail stress.

How stressful is marriage? In 1967, Thomas Holmes and Richard Rahe developed a rating scale that measures the number and magnitude of stressful life events that a person experiences. This scale is still commonly used today. Of the forty-one events listed on the scale, Holmes and Rahe found that marriage is the seventh most stressful life event. Marriage was rated to be more stressful than getting fired, retiring, and experiencing the death of a close friend. Of course, every person who marries does not experience the same amount of stress, as each person's interpretation of the marriage influences how stressful it becomes. Marriage *is* a major life event, and you will experience some stress along with this exciting transition.

Marriage produces many big and small changes over an extended period of time. Some of the bigger changes you may experience include moving to a new location, purchasing a home, changing your financial situation, and rearranging relationships with your and your partner's friends and family members. Other changes you may face include combining finances, accepting legal responsibility for one another, negotiating household responsibilities, and planning where to spend holidays. As changes arise, they can lead to chronic stress, which can put you at risk for developing physical health problems.

Each couple is unique in the amount of time it takes to adjust to marriage, and there is no guarantee that both partners will move at the same pace. Some couples' strong communication skills help them negotiate their differences quickly during the adjustment period. For other couples, each new change brings up new problems to be resolved, and the transition takes a bit longer. The common denominator for all couples as they enter marriage is change.

Adjusting to Change

Fortunately, all of this change doesn't have to be a bad thing for you or your relationship. In fact, my guess is that you *want* change in your life and your relationship. Otherwise, you would not have decided to get married. In this section, I discuss four strategies to help you ease the transition to married life: be aware of your tolerance for change, take on one change at a time, begin with acceptance of one another, and balance togetherness with your spouse with self-care.

Be Aware of Your Tolerance for Change

Some people love change and delight in every new transition they face. Monotony bores these people, who relish a life of uncertainty and uncharted adventure. Other people are creatures of habit who prefer stability. For them, change is difficult and even frightening. Most people are somewhere in the middle—enjoying new opportunities, but facing each new change with a bit of stress and worry about what is to come. Compare your level of change tolerance with your partner's tolerance for change in the following exercise.

Directions: On a scale of 1 to 10 (with 1 being very comfortable and 10 being quite uncomfortable), rate your tolerance for change as it relates to the following statements. Ask your partner to do the same. Notice how close or far apart your numbers are regarding how you each feel about change.

HOW DO YOU FEEL ABOUT CHANGE?

PARTNER A:

▶ I love change! Stability bores me.____

▶ I enjoy change, but I get somewhat nervous whenever I face any new transition. ____

▶ I wish I never had to experience change. Change makes me very anxious.____

PARTNER B:

▶ I love change! Stability bores me.____

▶ I enjoy change, but I get somewhat nervous whenever I face any new transition.____

▶ I wish I never had to experience change. Change makes me very anxious.____

Consider how comfortable you feel in the face of change to determine how much to prepare for the upcoming transitions you will experience in your marriage. Consider also your partner's attitudes toward change so you can be supportive during the adjustment to marriage. If your partner is less comfortable with change than you are, be patient as your partner adjusts to marriage. On the other hand, if your partner is more comfortable with change than you are, allow yourself more time to adjust to marriage. Communicate with your partner about how you can help each other deal with changes during the initial adjustment period in your marriage. One way to deal with the changes together is to develop a master "to-do" list of all the tasks that need to be done, and determine which ones can be done by one partner individually, and which will require the attention of both of you. In the face of this transition, remember to set aside time when you *won't* talk about all of the changes going on around you, so you can be refreshed when it's time to face new challenges.

Take on One Change at a Time

You may feel overwhelmed by all the new issues you face when you consider them all at once. Sometimes you may feel overwhelmed just by thinking of a few of the things you have to do that relate to your wedding and marriage. For example, at one point after I was married, I became stressed over the process of changing my name. Many steps are involved in this process, and my own legal name change was made more difficult because I was married in a different country. It seemed that there were an infinite number of places where I had to register my new name, and I quickly became overwhelmed by the many things I had to do to complete this task. The most effective way for me to change my name everywhere was to break down the larger job into smaller tasks. This way, each small task I completed was an accomplishment, and I could track my progress. Finally,

I resolved the task and assumed my new name (although some-how after years of marriage I *still* continue to receive credit card offers addressed to me using my maiden name—even after I've moved to a new state!).

Divide the changes you face into smaller tasks, and these changes will become more manageable. For example, suppose that you and your partner feel confused about changing your financial arrangements to meet the needs of your new marriage. Because there are so many details to your finances, you do not even know where to begin. If you divide your financial changes into several smaller steps, you can resolve each matter success-fully. First, you might decide that the financial changes you want to make include deciding who will be responsible for paying the bills, how much money you will spend each month, and which bank you will use. Next, you tackle each of these changes one by one. Soon, your overall financial arrangements have changed, and you were both involved in the decision-making process.

Taking each change as it comes helps minimize the stress of the overall transition to married life. You feel comfortable know-ing that each change is resolved successfully. You have more time to evaluate the potential consequences of each change, and you and your spouse are in a better position to move forward. Although you will face many changes when you get married, you do not need to handle them all at once. Focus on the changes that require your immediate attention first (such as filing any necessary legal paperwork), and be patient with yourselves as you take the time you need to get around to the lower-priority changes and tasks. Remember, you're committing to a lifetime together; there is no need to get everything done at once!

Begin with Acceptance of One Another

Many new spouses become disappointed with their partners, their relationships, or both when the initial infatuation wears off. During the courtship period, many couples hold idealized, romanticized images of each other. Although these images create excitement and passion, they also create disappointment when the real version of the partner comes into view. It is not usually the case that this real version of the partner did not exist before. Rather, this version was just not visible through the cloudy lenses of romance.

Partners sometimes blame each other for failing to meet unrealistic expectations. Partners often hold idealized images of what they want their spouses to be or do. When these expectations are not met, frustration and disappointment may result. Problems arise when spouses expect perfection from one another. For this reason, one of the major tasks that you and your partner must complete as you adjust to marriage is to accept each other *as you are*. Acceptance is a first step toward positive change in any relationship, and especially marriage.

Accepting your new spouse makes adjusting to marriage much, much easier for you. Without acceptance, you strive constantly to change your relationship into something it cannot be, or at least something that it is not yet ready to be. There are no easy secrets to developing acceptance for your partner. The best place to start is by looking into a mirror. Ask yourself, "Would I want my partner to hold me to the same standards I am using to judge him or her?" Your partner probably has some unrealistic expectations of you as well. You may need to talk with your partner about his or her unrealistic expectations if it appears that you are being judged according to an unfair standard. Make acceptance a top priority for your marriage.

Balance Togetherness with Your Spouse with Self-Care

Once married, you must define how you will live your life together. Any major decision you made individually in the past—such as where to live, where to work, or where to vacation—now needs to be discussed with another person, and your preferences won't prevail in every decision. This represents a major shift in the life of the marrying individual. My experience as a counselor has shown me that this transition can be especially difficult for individuals who have been living on their own for a long time and have enjoyed the independence they experienced through this living arrangement.

A significant task you face as you adjust to married life is balancing togetherness with personal independence. You must find a gentle balance between these two powerful forces. The desire for independence pushes you to a goal of self-preservation. You want to ensure that your opinions are heard and your ideas are appreciated. Simultaneously, a yearning for togetherness urges you to become inseparable from your partner, and you crave limitless intimacy. Both extremes pose serious risks to your well-being. Too much independence comes at the sake of closeness with your partner, while excessive togetherness leads to fusion and a lost identity. A balance must be reached.

Marriage involves a balance of self-care, your partner's care, and care for your relationship. Caring for yourself allows you to remain strong even when your partner's imperfections disappoint you. Caring for your partner helps your partner grow in positive ways. Caring for your relationship creates a safe environment in which both you and your partner feel comfortable when dealing with change. At times, it may seem that these needs are in conflict with one another. However, in the end, you will find that caring for yourself, your partner, and your relationship are the same thing.

Conclusion

The changes that come with marriage force you to make adaptations in your life. How prepared are you for those changes? You need not feel entirely ready for all of the changes you will face before you marry. Although change is stressful, it often leads to new, positive experiences. Join with your partner so these changes become a springboard for growth—for you and your relationship. In time, you may notice that your relationship no longer resembles what it was when you began. Strive for positive change!

Action Plan: Adjusting to Married Life

1. Expect that getting married will bring a number of related changes to your life and your relationship.

2. Examine your and your partner's typical levels of comfort in responding to life changes.

3. Manage one change at a time.

4. Build on a foundation of love and acceptance as you face changes related to your marriage.

5. Strive to maintain balance between caring for yourself and enjoying togetherness with your partner.

Discussion Questions

1. What do you think will be the biggest adjustments for you once you get married?

2. In what ways could marriage be stressful for you?

3. What do you think your partner will be surprised to learn about you after you are married?

4. How have you successfully managed major life changes before?

5. How can you support your partner as you go through the changes associated with getting married?

James and Chris have been married almost two years. Lately, they've become concerned that they can't find any time for sex. James and Chris hope that their sex life doesn't continue to deteriorate. The couple's limited sexual intimacy has caused a major strain on their relationship.

Both partners work late into the night at their jobs, and on the weekends they are so tired that they can barely drag themselves to do their weekend errands. Chris misses the intense sexual intimacy they shared in the early days of marriage. James feels that they are just temporarily out of step, but it will pass once they are established in their careers and current projects are complete.

For the first few months of their marriage, James and Chris used to make love about three times a week. Now, they have slipped to about one time every other week. Even when they are intimate, it lacks the passion it once had. "Maintenance sex," James calls it. Chris adds, "I guess this is just what happens when you get married."

eight
Your Sexual Relationship

Many couples hear the common myth that sex between married partners is boring, monotonous, and infrequent. Chris and James have become resigned to the fact that their sex life will never be as hot and passionate as it was early in their relationship. Although this couple is distressed by their decreased sexual intimacy, they seem to have made other areas of their lives into higher priorities—such as their careers and managing their household. They are like many couples, for whom the sexual relationship is one of the most common topics of their arguments in the early years of marriage.

Certainly, your sexual relationship will change during different stages of your marriage—in positive and negative ways. The great news is that—surprise!!!—it *is* possible to be married and have a satisfying sexual relationship with your partner. There are some wonderful books about keeping love alive in marriage, which you may wish to refer to after reading this chapter, such as *Hot Monogamy*, by Patricia Love and Jo Robinson, and *Secrets of a Passionate Marriage*, by David Schnarch. The key to a great sex life during marriage is not fancy tricks or wild sexual techniques. Rather, the best ways to maintain a satisfying sexual relationship are through effective communication and a solid relational connection between you.

There are many ways to have a healthy sexual relationship. The degree of passion and satisfaction in a marital sexual relationship cannot be measured by any simple number—such as the frequency of sexual intercourse, the amount of time spent in love-making, or the percentage of the time each partner has an orgasm during sex. Each couple has a unique approach to maintaining their sexual relationship. Decide what is right for you and use the time during your engagement to discuss your vision for your marital sexual relationship. This chapter will help you and your partner create strategies and goals to make and keep your sexual relationship a priority within your marriage.

This chapter focuses on helping you to communicate effectively with your partner about sex so you can increase your chances for a lifetime of satisfying, exciting sex. I explore some of the reasons that communicating about sex is uncomfortable. You'll also learn common myths about sexual communication. Then you'll discover strategies for enhancing sexual communication. This chapter helps you communicate about sex now, while you're engaged, so you can develop a satisfying sexual relationship once you are married.

Why Is Talking about Sex Uncomfortable?

Talking about sex can be difficult, even within the context of a marital or premarital relationship. Most people learn about sex from their parents, friends, and teachers. Early conversations about sex often focus on the basics, such as the physiology of sex, contraception, and moral values. Too often, these conversations fail to equip people with the skills they need to communicate effectively about sex with their partners. Also, many people discover as adults that much of the information they learned about sex as a child or adolescent was just plain wrong! Some early discussions are also surrounded by discomfort, which conveys the message that talking about sex is uncomfortable and embarrassing.

In addition to a lack of preparation for these conversations, other barriers may prevent you and your partner from feeling free to speak openly about sex. First, cultural barriers can inhibit people from talking about sex. Some cultural norms convey the message that communicating about sex is not appropriate in polite conversation. Second, many people are uncomfortable talking about sex because they fear that they lack knowledge. These people worry that their ignorance will be exposed when they talk about sex, and they do not want to appear naive or inexperienced to their partners. Third, many people are not honest about sex for fear of upsetting their partners. People often are extremely sensitive when it comes to sexual issues, such as when one partner does not enjoy the other partner's sexual techniques. Some people prefer to accept their circumstances rather than risk hurting their partners.

When sexual communication is difficult, partners avoid important conversations that could enhance their sexual intimacy. For many couples, avoiding the discomfort in discussing these issues is easier than facing the potential embarrassment that accompanies such a conversation. Couples that avoid these conversations miss important opportunities to strengthen their relationships.

Couples' sexual relationships can be powerful sources of increased intimacy and connection within their relationships. I encourage you not to miss out on the opportunity to develop this aspect of your relationship out of fear of speaking about it.

Myths about Sexual Communication

Further complicating the issue of sexual communication, some people hold common irrational beliefs that make it more difficult for them to talk about sex. Consider the following myths about sexual communication, and assess the degree to which you currently believe in them.

Myth #1: People Who Are in Love Should Find It Easy to Talk about Sex

Wouldn't life be great if romance was as easy to achieve and maintain as it appears in the movies? In the movies, lovers know all the right things to say and do. Their conversations about sex appear effortless and effective. Assuming you don't have writers to script your sexual conversations, discussions about sex in the "real world" are a bit stickier than those on the big screen. Even if you and your partner share a love that is as deep and passionate as any big-screen romance, you can't expect all of your conversations about sex to be easy. Conversations about sex are so difficult *because* you love your partner so deeply. Because of your intense love, respect, and concern for your partner, you do not want to hurt her or his feelings by suggesting that you are unsatisfied with your sexual relationship.

There is something romantic about the notions that "We can talk about everything," and "We know everything about each other." However, these ideas neglect the fact that love does not automatically erase all of the discomfort you feel in discussing sensitive topics within your relationship. Even people who are in love have their own thoughts and opinions on many issues, including sex. You can't assume you know all your partner's feelings and preferences.

Myth #2: Long-Term Partners Inherently Know How to Please Each Other

Often, people expect their partners to read their minds and know what they are thinking. Couples learn a lot about one another over time, and you may come to a point when you know a lot about your partner's sexual needs, preferences, and opinions. However, there are a few reasons to use caution when you make assumptions about your partner's thoughts. First, your partner may have been silent about his or her concerns for a long time. Some people are not comfortable talking about their sexual preferences unless they are asked directly, and even then it may be a struggle they choose to avoid. Second, both your and your partner's sexual desires change over time. Just because you know what pleases your partner now, there is no guarantee that she will feel the same way over time. Third, you can never be fully certain that you know exactly what your partner is thinking unless she tells you. Most married people continue to learn new things about their spouses after years of marriage.

Myth #3: The Best Time to Talk about One's Sexual Relationship Is in the Heat of Passion

Well, many people do not actually think that the heat of passion provides the "best" time for sexual conversations, but this is the time when many people raise issues related to sex. Some couples assume that talking about sex at this time is easier. I even know of couples that have never had a conversation about sex outside of their beds! There is no single best time to talk about sex, and it is possible to have effective conversations about sex during moments of passion. However, moments of passion do not provide the best opportunities for some types of sexual communication. When you discuss sexual concerns during passionate moments, you may forget to raise important issues, and you may fear discussing sensitive topics to avoid spoiling the romantic mood. You can communicate effectively about sex at many times. Figure out the most effective times for you and your partner to discuss your sexual relationship—both when it is going well and when one or both of you have concerns about it.

Myth #4: It Is Not "Ladylike" to Discuss Sex and Myth #5: A "Real Man" Should Just Know How to Please His Partner

Myths 4 and 5 describe some beliefs that people hold related to gender expectations about sexual communication. Certain assumptions exist about how men and women should communicate about sex. For example, women often believe that it is inappropriate for them to talk openly about sex. A double standard affects men as well. Often, men are assumed to be sexually knowledgeable and experienced. It is difficult for many people to leave these gender expectations behind, even within the context of a loving, intimate relationship. These gender expectations are often learned through your family of origin and at an early age. Discuss your beliefs about sexual communication and gender. The questions at the end of this chapter will help you begin this discussion.

Strategies for Effective Sexual Communication

You can overcome the barriers and myths that prevent you from communicating effectively about sex. Use the following strategies to enhance this area of your relationship.

Strategy #1: Talk about Talking about Sex

Discuss your feelings about sexual communication to understand each other's level of comfort with these issues. Think back to the earliest lessons you learned about sex and how those lessons continue to impact you today. Respect your partner's level of comfort, and demonstrate your willingness to work together to determine what is comfortable. Sometimes just broaching this topic is a challenge for couples. I suggest that you begin a dialogue about talking about sex with your partner by inviting them into this conversation with you. For example, you might say, "Honey, I'd like to spend some time talking with you about how we communicate about sex. I think we do a lot of things well, and I also think it would be interesting to learn more about how we each feel about talking about sex within our relationship." Other ways you can begin this conversation are by asking your partner how she learned about sex, finding out how his or her family talked about sex, and discussing the myths presented in this chapter.

Strategy #2: Maintain an Open Conversation about Sex with Your Partner

Talk about sex with your partner when things are going well. Talk about sex when things are not going well. Talk about sex when you are maintaining any changes you have made already in your sexual relationship. Don't put yourself in a situation in which the only time you talk about sex is when a problem exists. This situation leads you to believe that your sexual relationship is entirely bad. Rather than focusing only on the negative aspects, celebrate the strengths of your sexual relationship. (After all, who doesn't enjoy hearing that they are a good lover from time to time?)

Strategy #3: When You Make Requests of Your Partner, Be Clear and Specific—One Request at a Time

If you have a request of your partner to try something different sexually, identify the specific change you hope your partner will make. Once you are specific about your request, communicate your needs effectively. Find a time when your partner is willing to listen. Ask if your partner understands you. And, finally, do not overwhelm your partner by expecting her to make many major changes at once. It is easier to make one small change at a time. Then reinforce those changes when they occur.

Strategy #4: When Your Partner Makes Requests of You, Listen Carefully

Listen to your partner, and ensure that you understand his or her request. Be open to your partner's requests and consider them carefully. However, be honest about what you will or will not do. Neither of you should ever be pressured to do something sexually that you do not want to do. A satisfying sexual relationship is as much about setting limits as it is about exploring new possibilities.

Strategy #5: Take Time to Know Yourself, Your Partner, and Your Relationship

You and your partner will have a unique approach to communicating about sex, as well as unique preferences for the sexual activities you prefer or would like to try. As you consider your preferences for sexual communication and behavior, consider whether your present habits help or hinder you in creating the relationship that you desire. As you learn your partner's preferences, be sensitive to the differences between you. If your partner is less comfortable talking about sex than you are, be patient and support positive change. It takes time to become comfortable talking openly about sex—particularly if a person learns early in life that sex is not an acceptable topic for discussion. With increased comfort, you come closer to realizing your dreams for your sexual relationship.

Conclusion

James and Chris, the couple from the case study at the start of this chapter, can benefit from having more open discussions about their sexual relationship. If they are able to apply the strategies described in this chapter, they will become more aware of each other's preferences and desires. In addition, they can examine the cultural stereotypes that may be influencing their sexual relationship. Sexuality and intimacy are important points of connection for couples in their marriages. Therefore, James and Chris will benefit from working together to create a mutually satisfying sexual relationship that allows them to reconnect in the midst of their busy schedules.

You and your partner will define the type of sexual relationship you have once you are married. Your sexual relationship can be a fulfilling aspect of your relationship, which allows you to share one of the deepest forms of intimacy. On the other hand, sex is a common source of arguments and distress for newly married couples. This chapter explored the reasons that open communication about sex, even between married partners, is often difficult and uncomfortable. Use the strategies for effective sexual communication presented in this chapter, and work toward establishing a fulfilling sexual relationship. Your marriage does not need to relegate you to a lifetime of unsatisfying sex. Rather, your sexual relationship can provide closeness, passion, and intimacy that will grow throughout your marriage.

Action Plan: Your Sexual Relationship

1. Examine your personal level of comfort with talking about sex within your relationship.

2. Consider the extent to which you have been influenced by the commons myths about sexual communication that were presented in this chapter.

3. Build stronger communication about sex within your marriage by maintaining an open conversation, using sensitivity when making and receiving requests for your partner or you to change, and being patient with the process of developing and maintaining a satisfying sexual relationship with your spouse.

Discussion Questions

1. What kind of conversations did you have about sex in your family while you were growing up?

2. What do you think your parents believe about how men and women should communicate about sex?

3. What messages do the media convey about talking about sex?

4. What is one thing you and your partner could do to improve the way you talk about sex?

5. When are some times that you would feel most comfortable talking about sex?

6. What could you do to help your partner feel more comfortable talking about sex with you?

7. Which myths discussed in this chapter have been most influential on your attitudes toward talking about sex?

Robert and Janet married last month.

They both graduated recently from the same college in California. Robert is from Ohio, and Janet's family lives in Arizona. Right now, they are deciding where to start their life together. They are currently taking the summer off to enjoy their transition to marriage and make future career plans.

Robert wants to move to Ohio to be close to his family. He had a difficult time being far away from them while he was in college. His family is important to him, and he wants to live near them.

Janet prefers to move to the place where they find the best job opportunities. Although Janet's family is emotionally close, she wants to focus on establishing her and Robert's careers, even if they must live far away from their families.

Janet and Robert want to live somewhere they both can be happy. Both have received good job offers from companies in California. As they decide where to live, they feel tension between wanting to be close to Robert's family and taking the best career opportunities.

nine

Your Values

Married couples are often caught between two different sets of values. In Janet and Robert's situation, the struggle is between career and family. In your relationship, similar struggles may occur between values of independence and togetherness, planning for the future and having fun now, financial security and career satisfaction, and loyalty to your parents and loyalty to your spouse. Your values can provide you with clarity or confusion. In this chapter, I begin by discussing the role of values in your relationship. Next, I discuss the role that values play in marital conflict. Finally, I encourage you and your partner to draw upon shared values to sustain your marriage.

Values and Your Relationship

Your values represent the things that are important to you. Values are the guiding principles that influence your decisions about how to act. Values may relate to your expectations of relationships and how people should treat one another. They also relate to your individual priorities for your life. Because your values are important to you, they influence your life, behavior, and relationships. Complete the following exercise to determine the values that are most relevant to you.

Directions: Rate the importance of each of the following values on a scale of 1 (least important) to 10 (most important). Ask your partner to do the same.

PARTNER A	PARTNER B

▶ Independence:

_____   _____

▶ Friendship:

_____   _____

▶ Family:

_____   _____

▶ Financial success:

_____   _____

▶ Honesty:

_____   _____

▶ Education:

_____   _____

▶ Concern for the environment:

_____   _____

▶ Physical health:

_____   _____

▶ Security:

_____   _____

▶ Leisure:

_____   _____

▶ Achievement:

_____   _____

▶ A strong spiritual foundation:

_____   _____

▶ Helping others:

_____   _____

PARTNER A	PARTNER B

▶ Concern for world peace:

_____   _____

▶ A good work ethic:

_____   _____

▶ Happiness:

_____   _____

▶ Physical attractiveness:

_____   _____

▶ Power:

_____   _____

▶ Excitement:

_____   _____

▶ Self-respect:

_____   _____

▶ A love of travel:

_____   _____

▶ Cultural diversity:

_____   _____

▶ Physical fitness:

_____   _____

▶ Religion/spirituality:

_____   _____

▶ Love:

_____   _____

Put a star by any value that you rated as eight or higher. These values
are most important to you, and they probably shape your thoughts and
behaviors. Compare your top values with those of your partner. Discuss
how similarities and differences might influence your marriage.

Many influences shape a person's values. The source of one's values may be parents, religion, the media, and peers. Cultural factors also influence values, although all members of the same culture do not necessarily share the same values. Go back to the previous exercise and look at the values you rated as most important. Where did you learn to value those things? Also, how have your values changed over time?

Values affect the manner in which you live your life. Your values will affect your marital relationship as well. Values influence your relationship in three ways: your choice of a spouse, the type of relationship you desire, and your behaviors within your relationship.

Your Choice of a Spouse

You selected your partner—out of the billions of people on the planet—to be the person with whom you want to spend your life. Why? Your values influenced your selection of a life partner. When dating, people seek certain qualities in partners. These are the characteristics they value in a person with whom they hope to share a relationship. Look in any personal ad. You'll find a request that looks something like this: "Seeking attractive, fun-loving partner who enjoys the outdoors and music." That brief statement is packed with values—physical attractiveness, fun and leisure, nature, and music. Most people value certain basic characteristics in a partner—such as kindness, shared interests, and honesty. Each person also has a unique set of values for qualities in a partner. Your values for a partner shaped your selection of your partner as your future spouse. Look back to the values you rated highly in the previous exercise. In what ways does your partner embody those values?

The Type of Relationship You Desire

Cultural norms and values influence your expectations about marriage. For example, marriages in a culture that values egalitarian relationships are different from marriages in a culture that values a submissive role for wives. Other value differences influence marriage as well. For instance, a couple whose primary values for their relationship are stability and security differs from a couple whose primary values are passion and romance. Of course, stability and passion are not mutually exclusive, and stable, passionate relationships exist. The values that are most important to you will help to shape your marriage in a unique way. Consider the potential influence of your values on your relationship.

Your Behaviors within Your Relationship

Values provide the background for human behavior. People strive to act in accordance with their values. Of course, they are not always successful, and some actions are not consistent with values. For the most part, however, your values guide your actions. The influence of values on behaviors is especially relevant in relationships. Do you value honesty? You will try to be honest with your partner. Do you value independence? You will attempt to maintain separate interests and friends outside of your marriage. Do you value romance? You will try to create romantic experiences with your partner.

Your values influence your relationship on many levels—in your choice of a mate, in the relationship qualities you desire, and in your actions toward your partner. Become aware of the values that shape your life and relationship. Understand the values that are important to your partner, and discuss with your partner the influence of values on your relationship. Knowledge of your partner's values helps you understand his or her behaviors, attitudes, and expectations for marriage. In addition, your values provide an important clue into the type of relationship you desire for the future.

When Values Collide

Perhaps a more suitable heading for this section is "When What You *Think* You Are Fighting about Is Not *Really* What You Are

Fighting About." Many conflicts stem from conflicting cultural norms and values. It may appear that you and your partner are fighting about where to go on vacation, but the fight is *really* about conflicting values for relaxation and adventure. Or it may seem that your argument is about the amount of money you'll spend on a new car, but the argument is *really* about different values for luxury and financial security. Value conflicts disguise themselves in many forms and contribute to many arguments between married partners.

Value conflicts are particularly challenging for couples when one or both partners feels that their values are threatened. People feel attacked or disrespected when they perceive that their partners do not honor their values. In many ways, your values define who you are. If you feel your partner does not respect your values, you may also feel that your partner does not respect *you*. This spells trouble in a marital relationship. Couples that seek out counseling often find that they are better able to resolve conflicts when they stop focusing on the surface-level issues and begin to look beneath the surface to discover the value conflicts that underlie their current disagreements.

Consider the following situation: Tina and Zack disagree about where to spend their first holiday season since their wedding (which is a *very* common challenge for newlywed couples). Zack wants to celebrate quietly at home together because he and Tina have little time for each other during their usual work week. Zack thinks that elaborate holiday plans would create more stress in their hectic schedules. Tina wants to celebrate with her family in her hometown, which is several hundred miles away. Tina misses her family and views the holiday vacation as the only opportunity to see her family in the near future.

On the surface, it appears that the disagreement between Tina and Zack relates to where to spend the holidays. Beneath the surface, however, a major value conflict exists. Zack values time alone with Tina, while Tina values time with her family.

Although each partner probably values time together as a couple and time with family members, Tina and Zack place differing levels of priority on each of these values. Both partners feel that their values are threatened. Zack thinks Tina doesn't care if they spend time together as a couple. Tina thinks that her family is not important to Zack. If this couple does not recognize the values underlying this conflict, this disagreement could spiral into a major fight.

Working Through Value Conflicts

What can Tina and Zack do? And what can you do if you are in a similar situation? Couples *can* work through value conflicts. The first and most important step is to become aware of the values that underlie the conflict. When you are in conflict with your partner, ask yourself, "What do I hope to gain from my argument?" Identify the meaning behind the resolution you seek. More than one value may be present in any conflict. For example, in an argument over household responsibilities (e.g., who will scrub the bathroom floor), you may value support from your partner *and* equality in household responsibilities.

Once you identify the values underlying your conflict, you are in a better position to negotiate and compromise. There are usually multiple solutions that would honor each partner's values. In Tina and Zack's conflict, for example, the couples could agree to visit her family for a few days and spend the rest of the vacation alone. Or they could commit to visiting her family at another time of year and enjoy the holiday alone. Take a step back from the conflict to create room for negotiation and change. There are often several paths to the same outcome, which is known as *equifinality*.

When you face a value conflict, understand the values that influence your partner's position. When you understand your partner's values, you become more sympathetic and less defensive. You may discover that your partner intends to enhance your relationship and look out for your well-being; he just has different ideas about how to go about doing so. Your partner's ideas about how to realize each of your values will often differ from your own ideas. This doesn't mean that either one of you is wrong; it just means that you have your own opinions. Ask your partner, "What do you hope to gain from your argument?" Determine the values behind his or her side of the argument. Then work toward a solution that accounts for the values that are important to both of you.

Conclusion

When your values are compatible with your spouse's values, your marriage provides you with fulfillment. You and your partner are joined in a mutual mission. Through this mission, decision-making is clear, and you unite in a shared purpose in life. Your marriage is defined by the values you share, and your shared values provide a foundation on which your daily lives are constructed. Develop shared values to help sustain your relationship, even during difficult times. Begin by finding common ground in your individual values. Which values do you and your partner share? You do not need to share every single value with your spouse. Having some unique values helps you each contribute new ideas and experiences to the relationship. However, when you identify the values you share, shape your marriage around these values.

What qualities would you each like to describe your marriage? In Chapter 1, you created a Marital Vision Statement. Look back to this statement now to identify the marriage-related values that you and your partner hold. Notice any other values you have for marriage that you did not include in this statement. Continue to explore your values for your marriage by considering the dreams you each hold for the future.

Action Plan: Your Values

1. Develop a clear understanding of the values that are important to you and your partner.

2. Be aware for situations in which value conflicts underlie disagreements between you and your partner.

3. Develop a core set of shared values to sustain your relationship.

Discussion Questions

1. What is most important to you in life?

2. How do your values guide the decisions you make?

3. How similar are your values to your partner's values?

4. What are the major differences between your and your partner's values?

5. What can you and your partner do if you are in a situation where your values conflict?

Paul and Jennie have been married for one year. They enjoyed their first year of marriage and feel satisfied with their relationship. Both Paul and Jennie work as teachers in the local school district.

Growing debt is a major stressor for the couple. Both partners feel stressed about their debt, and the couple is unsure how to pay off their bills. They have had a few minor disagreements related to their finances, but they now want to work together to build a solid financial foundation for their marriage.

The couple explains that their debt is a result of wedding expenses, recent unanticipated travel costs, and the expense of moving into a new apartment together. They never seem to have enough money coming in to cover all of their expenses.

Paul and Jennie share many goals for their future—such as buying a house—which require a sound financial situation. However, at this point, they don't know how to solve their financial problems.

ten
Problem-Solving Skills

Not all of the problems you face in marriage result from differences between you and your partner. Sometimes, you face problems together. Like Paul and Jennie, many couples face challenging problems in the early years of marriage—financial problems, conflict with family members, or career-related problems. You and your partner may also share other stressful experiences—such as coping with a family member's illness or moving to another city or state. Problems can enter your relationship in many shapes and forms. Your effectiveness in handling the problems you face as a couple influences the future of your relationship.

Times of stress and crisis present opportunities for you and your partner to grow closer together or further apart. This chapter presents several strategies for solving problems and coping with difficult situations. This chapter outlines a nine-step problem-solving model that you can use to address the unique problems that arise in your marriage. We will use the nine steps to examine and help Paul and Jennie resolve their financial struggles. This couple's experience shows how to apply the problem-solving model to your relationship.

Step 1: Identify the Problem

Before you can resolve a problem, you have to know what the problem is. Although this seems simple, problems are often more complex than they appear. In their original form, most problems are not defined clearly. As we saw in the Chapter 9, value conflicts are sometimes at the heart of a problem. Many people attempt to solve one problem when it would be more effective to solve another problem. When you face a challenging situation, carefully consider every aspect of the situation and work to resolve the problem in a way that will produce the most positive outcomes. You could waste a lot of time and energy trying to fix the wrong problem, which will not produce the desired outcome. You and your partner should agree on the general definition of the problem. You cannot work together to solve a problem if you conceptualize the nature of the problem differently. If you disagree greatly in the way you each define the problem, you may actually be trying to solve two problems at once. In this case, focus on one problem at a time until both are resolved.

Consider the situation of Paul and Jennie. They identified the problem that their income never covers their monthly expenses. However, the *real* problem may be that the couple has extravagant spending habits. If Paul and Jennie attempted to solve their problem by trying to increase their income, while the real problem was out-of-control spending habits, they would not resolve their financial problems. For our purposes, we will assume that Paul and Jennie identified the correct problem: They do not make enough money to cover their basic expenses. Once they identify their problem, they are ready to move on to the next step.

Step 2: Examine the Problem

Examine the details of the problem to gain a deeper understanding of the situation. Consider the following questions: Who is involved? What are the important details of the problem? What chain of events led to the creation of this problem? How do you know that it is a problem for you? At this stage, try to develop detailed knowledge about the problematic situation. This information allows you to expand your view of the problem and your range of available solutions.

Paul and Jennie decided to face the facts and important details about their financial problems. They uncovered several things during this exploration. First, the amount of their monthly rent equaled about one-half of their total monthly income. Second, the amount of money they paid monthly toward their credit card debt did not cover the amount they were charged in interest. Third, they had no record of their expenses, and they never maintained a budget. All of these details helped Paul and Jennie understand the problem in greater detail.

Step 3: Consider What You Have Done to Solve the Problem in the Past

Consider what you did in the past to try to solve the problem you face now. People often attempt many solutions before they discover an effective solution to a particular problem. Often past attempted solutions contain important clues for how to solve the current problem. Before you develop new solutions, review the solutions you attempted previously.

Jennie and Paul examined what they did previously to try to solve their financial problems. One strategy they used was spending less money on entertainment. For example, they rented movies instead of going to a movie theater, and they sought out inexpensive social events when they spent time with friends. A second strategy they used was asking their parents for financial help. When a financial emergency arose, one of the partners called his or her parents and requested a loan to cover the unexpected costs.

Step 4: Evaluate the Effectiveness of Past Solutions

Not all solutions are effective at solving a problem. Once you identify the solutions you attempted previously, evaluate the effectiveness of each one. Sometimes a solution works very well, and you can reapply the same strategy. Other times, a solution is ineffective and not worth continuing. In still other situations, a solution is partially effective but does not eliminate the problem. Also, evaluate the effectiveness of solutions you used when you faced *similar* problems in the past, even if they do not relate directly to the current problem. Understanding the effectiveness of previous solutions can help you to develop strategies to resolve the problem you face now.

Paul and Jennie considered the effectiveness of the two solutions they applied previously to their financial problems. First, they evaluated the effectiveness of cutting back their entertainment expenses. They decided that this was an effective strategy in reducing their expenses but not in producing enough extra cash to eliminate their debt. Second, they evaluated the effectiveness of asking for financial assistance from their parents. They decided this was not an effective strategy for several reasons. First, it increased their debt because they owed money to their parents. Second, it strained their relationships with their parents when they could not repay the money quickly. Finally, they did not feel right about borrowing money from their parents, as they desired financial independence. Once they considered the relative merits of their previous solutions, they decided which solutions to revisit (cutting entertainment expenses) and avoid in the future (asking their parents for loans).

Step 5: Brainstorm

Brainstorming involves developing new ideas for solutions without judging the value of those ideas. When you brainstorm, suspend judgment of your ideas, even when they seem totally crazy. Many people judge ideas prematurely. This contributes to misjudging ideas and creates an environment in which new ideas are not freely expressed. Solutions are not always logical, so be open to all of the ideas that you and your partner develop. You never know when an idea will contain the solution to your problem, so let your ideas flow. The more possible solutions you generate, the more likely you will be to strike on one that works.

When Paul and Jennie brainstormed a list of possible solutions to their financial problems, they came up with many ideas. Their list included meeting with a financial planner, moving to a less expensive apartment, moving in with one of their parents temporarily while they saved up money and paid down their debt, creating and sticking to a budget, taking on extra part-time jobs, consolidating their debt with a nonprofit credit counseling service, and cutting down their spending habits by eliminating unnecessary expenses. Many of these ideas relate directly to the details of the problem they discovered in the second step. At this stage, Jennie and Paul's goal was to develop a complete list, without judging their ideas. After creating a comprehensive list, the couple felt excited about their possibilities for solving their financial problems.

Step 6: Review Your Ideas and Choose One to Try

Of course, every idea generated during the brainstorming phase is not a good or practical solution. Once you exhaust all the possible ideas that may arise, identify the ideas that are most likely to contain the solution to your problem. Look over your list and cross off ideas that do not seem possible or desirable. Consider the resources available to you, and determine which ideas are realistic. Also, consider the solutions that are suitable to your personal strengths. Create a plan you can perform well. Finally, select one idea or a combination of ideas to implement. Select the solution that is most desirable to you and your partner.

When Paul and Jennie looked back through their list of possible solutions, they immediately crossed off three ideas. First, they did not want to take on extra jobs because they both felt overscheduled already. Second, they did not want to move to a less expensive apartment because they enjoyed their current home and did not want to go through another move. Third, they did not want to move in with one of their parents because they believed this option would create too much stress on their marriage and their relationships with their parents. Next, they decided that they were not able to afford the services of a financial planner at the current time, so they crossed that idea off of their list. After reviewing the remaining options, they decided to create a budget to track their expenses and raise awareness of their spending habits. They decided to develop this budget together so they would both agree to the plan.

Step 7: Experiment with This Idea

Once you decide on a solution, put it into action. Trial and error is often the best way to discover an effective solution to a problem. Don't expect to find the best solution to your problem on the first try—although you will increase your chances of doing so by planning carefully to implement your chosen solution. At this point, just implement some plan of action that seems likely to bring you closer to a solution. Think of this stage as an experiment, or a test, to see what happens when you try out your idea. It may work, and it may not work. Your goal right now is to act.

Jennie and Paul began to work on their budget. First, they spent a week tracking their expenses. They then set limits on their expenses for groceries, entertainment, and clothing. They also cut out some unnecessary expenses—such as cable television, extra telephone features, and dining out. Much to their surprise, they cut their monthly expenses by about $200, which created extra money to pay down their debts.

Step 8: Evaluate the Effectiveness of the Current Solution

After you give your solution an adequate testing period, evaluate its effectiveness. Ask yourselves, "How well has our solution worked?" Be honest about your progress. If your solution worked, then you can stop at this step and continue to maintain the effective solution. In other words, keep on doing what you have been doing. If your solution was wholly or partially ineffective, consider how productively you implemented the solution. Your problems may not have been resolved because you did not follow through on your original plans. In this case, reconsider whether the original plan was feasible and whether you should give it another try. If it seems like a second try with your original solution is destined to failure, accept that it did not work, and move on to the next step.

After three months on their budget, Jennie and Paul evaluated the effectiveness of their new spending plan. They were happy with the progress they made using the budget, which was allowing them to feel more in control over their financial situation. However, they believed that they were not paying enough on their debt each month to pay it off quickly. The high interest rates on their credit cards made it difficult to make real progress toward paying off their debt. Although they were happy with their budget and planned to continue living by it, they doubted it would be enough to reach their financial goals.

Step 9: Modify or Change the Solution If Necessary

If the strategy you tried did not produce an effective solution, re-evaluate your original decision. Decide whether you should modify or abandon your original plans. If a plan is not working, figure out what you can do differently. You learn more about the problem as you implement your solution, so you are in a better position to figure out a solution that will work. Revisit the list of ideas you created during the brainstorming session. Develop new ideas, and add those to the list. Then, choose a new strategy to use this time. You may need simply to make a few small changes to your original plan. If your original plan was totally ineffective, you need to create a new plan. You may need to cycle through this last step several times before you discover the best solution. Celebrate your progress when you solve your problem, because you will have worked hard to get to that point.

Paul and Jennie's budget was partially effective at helping them reach their financial goals. They kept the budget and added another strategy to intensify their efforts. They reviewed the list of solutions generated during their original brainstorming session. They decided to use a nonprofit credit consolidation service to negotiate a lower interest rate on their loans. Once they combined these two solutions—using a budget and working with a credit consolidation service—Jennie and Paul began to see real progress toward paying off their debt and saving to buy a house.

Conclusion

When you and your partner face problems, you may feel bogged down by the details of your situation. Focusing on the details of your problem can be overwhelming. Another approach you can use is to focus all of your attention on finding solutions. When you focus on solutions, you think less about the cause of the problem and more about strategies to make the situation better. Rather than asking, "What is wrong?" you can ask, "What can we do differently to change the situation?" In other words, how can you make the situation right?

Before problems arise, identify resources that you could use to help you solve problems. Gather together many possible sources of support. Consider people to whom you can turn for support, community resources, financial or material resources, and your and your partner's personal qualities that can help you during difficult times. A research study that I conducted with about 400 individuals currently involved in intimate relationships demonstrated that, in general, individuals who reported more resources available to support their relationships also demonstrated higher levels of relationship satisfaction. When you face problems that affect your relationship, support one another. Develop coping skills to help you deal with difficult situations.

In your quest for solutions, both partners generally must want to solve a problem to be able to find a mutually satisfying solution. When your problems affect both of you, new problems can arise when a partner does not participate in the problem-solving process. Although one partner can independently create positive change within a relationship, the other partner can easily thwart the efforts of the partner working to improve the relationship. Therefore, try to work together to solve the problems that affect your relationship.

Solving problems helps you and your partner develop intimacy and closeness. Your relationship becomes stronger when you overcome problems together. As you work together, you learn about each other, and you develop a resilient connection to your partner. Each new problem resolved successfully represents another victory for your relationship. Problem-solving skills are essential to building a lasting, supportive marriage. Develop these skills and be prepared for the problems you'll face once you are married.

Action Plan: Nine Steps to Solving Your Problems

- Step One: Identify the problem.

- Step Two: Examine the problem.

- Step Three: Consider what you have done to solve the problem in the past.

- Step Four: Evaluate the effectiveness of past solutions.

- Step Five: Brainstorm to come up with solutions.

- Step Six: Review your ideas and decide on one to try.

- Step Seven: Experiment with this idea.

- Step Eight: Evaluate the effectiveness of the current solution.

- Step Nine: Modify or change the solution if necessary.

Discussion Questions

1. Think of a problem you and your partner faced in your relationship in the past. How did you handle that problem?

2. If you could return to the time when you faced that problem, would you do anything differently to resolve the problem more effectively? If so, what?

3. What characteristics of your relationship will help you and your future spouse solve problems in marriage?

4. What do you anticipate will be the most difficult challenges you will face with your partner in the early years of your marriage?

5. What do you think are your partner's strengths in managing problems and coping with stress?

Both Dan and Stephanie were raised by Methodist parents, but neither one attends church on a regular basis anymore. They will be married in a church, and they are required to attend premarital counseling sessions with the pastor as well.

As Dan and Stephanie meet with the pastor, Dan begins to think that he would like to start to go to church again. He remembers how much he enjoyed the people in the church, and he wants to explore his faith again. He has already begun to read the Bible on his own, and he plans to start attending services regularly.

When Dan tells Stephanie of his desire to start going to church, she says, "I'll support you in that, but I'm not interested in going with you. I think it's great that you want to go, though."

Dan appreciates Stephanie's support to go back to church, although he is disappointed that she is not interested in joining him. He wonders how exploring his faith will affect their relationship, especially if Stephanie never joins him.

eleven
Religion and Spirituality

What role will religion and spirituality play in your marriage? How important are these things to you, and how much influence will they have on your relationship? Like Dan and Stephanie, you and your partner may not agree completely on matters of religion and spirituality. While you are planning your marriage, consider the influence of these issues on your future plans. In this chapter, you will consider the role of religion and spirituality in your life, and how this influences your relationship.

For most people, marriage is both a religious and a legal arrangement. In most religious traditions, marriage represents a sacred union that is sanctioned by a religious authority. In addition, marriage is a legal contract between two partners, which confers rights and responsibilities on spouses. Today, most couples still get married in religious institutions, so most couples have at least some spiritual foundation for their marriages. Even couples that choose nonreligious settings (e.g., outdoors or in a banquet facility) for their wedding ceremonies often include some type of religious or spiritual component to the wedding.

I begin this section with a discussion of spiritual development. Next, I ask you to consider the role spiritual issues will play in your relationship. Finally, I address considerations for partners with different religious backgrounds.

Spirituality and Religion

Religion and spirituality are distinct, yet related, entities. Spirituality is a universal experience of connectedness to a spiritual being, other people, nature, and mystical experiences. Religions are organized forms of spirituality in which groups of people share common beliefs, practices, and traditions. Within the same religious groups, people may express their spirituality differently. Both religion and spirituality are inextricably linked to a person's culture. Your and your partner's religious and spiritual backgrounds influence your core beliefs about life and your relationship. Consider which spiritual and religious beliefs and practices you share with your partner, and consider the differences between you in these areas. Then discuss the impact that your spirituality and/or religion have had on your relationship.

Spiritual and religious growth and development take many forms. Spiritual development represents a process, or journey, in which a person grows through his or her beliefs and practices. People commonly change their spiritual beliefs as they have new experiences, learn new lessons, and question the world around them. The spiritual beliefs you hold now are probably different from the beliefs you held ten years ago and from the beliefs you will hold ten years in the future. As you grow and change, you may come to think differently about life, the world around you, and your spiritual beliefs.

It would be wonderful if you and your partner could share all the same spiritual beliefs and travel together on the spiritual and religious journey of life. However, because you and your future spouse have had different life experiences, you each probably have a unique spiritual and/or religious outlook on life, even if you share many of the same fundamental beliefs. The path of your spiritual growth will differ from your partner's path, although your paths are linked. The challenge you face in marriage is supporting your partner's spiritual growth as you enhance your own spiritual development. Complete the following exercise to examine the past, present, and future course of your spiritual development.

Directions: On a separate sheet of paper, draw a picture representing your spiritual journey. Be creative. Your drawing may be literal or symbolic. Use crayons or colored pencils to enhance your picture. Include important influences on your spiritual beliefs—such as events, people, and experiences. Include you past and current experiences and your hopes for the future of your journey.

Ask your partner to create a picture representing his or her spiritual journey, using the previous guidelines. Once you have both completed your pictures, show and describe them to one another. Discuss the following questions:

- What did you learn about each other in seeing each other's pictures?

- What similarities are there between the spiritual journeys you have each taken?

- What differences are there between the spiritual journeys you have each taken?

- How compatible are your hopes and expectations for the future of your spiritual journeys?

The Spiritual Side of Your Marriage

How will you and your partner acknowledge the religious and spiritual side of your marriages, if at all? What role do you expect that religion and spirituality will play in your daily lives? If you plan to become parents or one or both of you already have children, how will you integrate your spirituality into your parenting practices? For some couples, religious values play a central role in shaping their marriage. Other couples do not focus on religion or spirituality at all. Still other couples fall in the middle of these extremes. Two of the main avenues through which spirituality and religion may influence your marriage include your social support network and your sexual relationship.

For many couples, practicing the same religious faith provides a social network to support their marriages. Religious institutions often promote healthy marriages within their communities. For example, many religious organizations offer premarital counseling and marriage education classes. Other religious organizations provide child care so couples with children can share time engaged in religious and social activities. Couples also meet other married couples through their religious organizations, which connects them to a social network that shares common values and beliefs. Couples not affiliated with a religious organization may need to work harder to create similar opportunities.

A social support network based on religious or spiritual beliefs may alter the manner in which couples define their relationships. In some religious traditions, marriage brings new opportunities and expectations to the partners. Couples learn that their marriage is important not only to themselves, but to the community to which they belong. Therefore, married couples sometimes define their relationships based on their roles within their religious community. If you and your partner are not already members of a religious or spiritual community, I encourage you to consider becoming affiliated with a group that is in accordance with your beliefs and values. If you and your partner are of different faiths, you may wish to join different communities, as will be discussed further in the next section. However, couples wishing to join together should take all the time they need to seek out a spiritual community that is comfortable to them. My husband and I visited numerous churches before finally settling on one that we really enjoy when we last moved to a new hometown. The time you spend visiting different organizations will help you to clarify your expectations and needs, expose you to different forms of spiritual practice, and provide opportunities for communication and learning about your partner.

Spirituality and Sexuality

Religious and spiritual organizations not only provide social support to married couples, but they also shape individuals' morals and values in marriage. This is particularly true for a couple's sexual relationship, as religion often influences an individual's beliefs and expectations about sexuality. Your religious upbringing probably influenced your beliefs about sexuality. Your religious or spiritual beliefs may stipulate with whom you should or should not have a sexual relationship, the type of contraception you should use, and the nature of sex between married partners. Because your spiritual beliefs are closely related to your beliefs about sex, explore the influence your beliefs have had on your sexuality.

Sexuality and spirituality are also linked through the spiritual connection many couples experience in their sexual relationship. The intimacy spouses share provides opportunities for spiritual unity and growth. As couples develop sexual intimacy, they come to a deeper understanding of the spiritual connections between people. Likewise, many spouses find that their sexual relationship is most fulfilling when they share similar spiritual beliefs. Explore the spiritual influences on your relationship. You may find that journaling, speaking with a religious advisor or other spiritual mentor, and spending time in prayer or meditation help you with this exploration. Consider the role spirituality and religion will play in your marriage, and talk about these issues with your partner. Discuss with your partner how you can strengthen the spiritual side of your relationship. Your relationship may move to a deeper level as you acknowledge the spiritual connection you share.

Partners of Different Faiths

Marriages between partners of different religious faiths are increasingly common. In this section, I discuss some issues that you and your partner may face if you are in this situation. Again, even partners who share the same religious background may have some differences in their spiritual beliefs. Also, one or both partner's religious beliefs could change over time. You might share the same beliefs when you marry, but your beliefs become different over time.

Spiritual differences are especially relevant for couples in which the partners come from different religious orientations. For example, one partner is Jewish, and the other is Roman Catholic. Perhaps one person is Protestant, and his or her partner is an atheist. Partners of different faiths can have successful marriages, and religious differences do not signify a doomed marriage. In fact, I have met many long-lasting couples in which partners belong to different religious organizations, or one partner attends but the other does not. It is, however, important in these situations for couples to be proactive in discussing their differences and creating a practice that works for them in their relationships. Otherwise, religious differences can become a source of stress for married couples.

Partners of different faiths face some unique struggles that would not occur if the partners shared the same religious background. One reason that having different religious backgrounds presents so many challenges is that a person's religion is closely related to one's moral beliefs, understanding of the world, and family relationships. Sometimes, direct conflicts between partners' religious beliefs create tension in the relationship. Religious differences also indirectly create conflicts when different expectations about the marital relationship, traditions, and religious practices arise.

Early in their relationships, interfaith couples should discuss the religious and cultural traditions they expect to continue in their marriages. Religious traditions and holidays are unique challenges for interfaith couples, especially when they involve dietary or behavioral restrictions. Discuss the celebration of holidays in your marriage. Create an arrangement that respects each partner's faith. For example, a couple may decide to celebrate all holidays jointly, to the extent possible within each partner's faith. Another couple may decide that each partner celebrates only the religious holidays of his or her religion, but they celebrate all nonreligious holidays together.

Having children often brings issues of religious differences to the forefront. Arrangements that work for a childless couple become complicated when children enter the relationship. In some instances, both partners (and their parents) will want to raise the children in their own religious faith. Alternatively, other couples decide to expose the children to both religious traditions and let the child decide, but they do not want to confuse the child with theological differences. Discuss your expectations with your partner before you have children. Consult with each partner's clergyperson and consider this input when you discuss this matter.

You and your partner may be entirely comfortable with your religious differences. However, everyone else in your life may not feel the same way. Interfaith couples sometimes find that their families have more trouble with their different religions than they do. Family members may view your marriage as a threat to their legacy, or even a betrayal of the manner in which you were raised. Family members are not the only ones who may be uncomfortable with your religious differences. Friends, clergy, fellow believers, and even coworkers may not approve. Even those people who approve of your relationship probably have many questions for you. They may wonder how you celebrate holidays, if you will continue to practice your faith, and how you will raise children. Because you may face disapproval or questioning, reflect on your personal commitment to the relationship and work together to handle religious differences between you. Discuss how you can respond to questions from disapproving or curious family members and friends. Also, develop clear ideas about how you will integrate religious traditions into your new marriage—or create new traditions—so you'll be prepared to describe your choices and plans to the people around you. Finally, be prepared to change the topic of conversation or politely decline to answer questions when you would prefer to keep your beliefs private.

Conclusion

Marriage presents opportunities for spiritual connection and growth. Religion and spirituality are sensitive issues, so be respectful of your partner as you consider the role that spirituality will play in your marriage. When you marry, you join formally with your partner in a continual process of spiritual growth and development. As much as you are able, strive to support your partner in his or her spiritual growth. Pay attention to the spiritual side of your marriage, and create opportunities to deepen your spiritual connection to one another. Although religious and spiritual differences may present challenges for your marriage, managing these differences helps you further your development and strengthen your relationship. Marriage is a spiritual bond between you and your spouse, so seek out opportunities to fortify that bond.

Action Plan: Religion and Spirituality

1. Reflect upon your religious and spiritual development to identify the people and experiences that have influenced you.

2. Consider the manner in which your religious faith and spirituality will influence your future marriage.

3. If you and your partner are of different faiths, talk about the religious and spiritual traditions and practices you wish to include in your marriage.

Discussion Questions

1. How important would you like religion and spirituality to be in your marriage?

2. What could your partner do to support you in your spiritual growth?

3. What roles have spirituality and religion played in your relationship so far?

4. Where could you turn if you were seeking spiritual guidance?

5. In what ways are your religious and spiritual beliefs similar to and different from your partner's beliefs? How might these similarities and differences influence your marriage?

Simone and Greg have been married for just over six months. They lived apart until they married, so living together has been an adjustment.

The partners differ in their preferences for cleanliness in the home. Simone prefers clean surroundings, while Greg is a self-proclaimed slob. This difference has been the source of several disagreements.

Their disagreements center on their expectations about household responsibilities. Greg believes that Simone should be responsible for cleaning because she has such high standards. Simone believes that she can't do all of the work herself, especially if Greg does not cooperate with her and creates even more of a mess than she does.

Greg made efforts to be clean but feels that Simone is never happy with the results. Simone is frustrated and irritated because she feels that she must constantly clean up after Greg.

They both wonder, "Will we ever be able to agree on this issue?"

twelve

Gender Role Expectations and Household Tasks

The key question we consider in this chapter is, "Who will do what, when, and how?" That simple-sounding question causes many couples a great deal of stress and frustration—just like Simone and Greg are experiencing. In fact, the distribution of household labor is one of the most common topics of early marital disagreements. The division of household tasks creates problems when one or both of the partners is not satisfied with the agreed-upon arrangement. The expectations that each person holds about which gender is best suited for certain types of activities complicate the division of household labor. Many couples today strive for gender equality and an equal division of labor. However, even couples with the egalitarian values often experience difficulties in implementing their value for equality on a practical level.

This chapter addresses issues related to gender role expectations and household tasks. First, you will consider the sources of your expectations about gender roles and household tasks. Next, we address the complicated issue of dividing household tasks. Finally, I discuss strategies to avoid a never-ending battle over housework.

Where Do Your Expectations Come From?

The term *gender role expectations* describes the beliefs and expectations an individual holds in regard to what activities a person of a particular gender should and should not do. Gender role expectations often influence the problems that married couples face. Gender role expectations also impact partners' needs for intimacy, emotional expressiveness, and relationship patterns. In addition, communication patterns, relationships with friends, and the sexual relationship often reflect the gender identities and expectations of each spouse. However, perhaps the most significant area in which gender role expectations can cause problems is the division of household tasks.

A lot of time, energy, and resources are required to keep a household in working order. In this chapter, I use the term *household tasks* to refer to much more than cooking and cleaning. The jobs required to run a household include other duties—managing the finances and paying the bills (which is addressed in Chapter 13), making household improvements, yard work, running errands, buying groceries and household supplies, caring for pets, scheduling appointments, and caring for children. Many other specific jobs may be required to maintain your particular household.

Every person is a product of the environment in which he or she was raised. The customs people learn early in their lives about gender-appropriate household activities are difficult to release in adulthood. Examine your expectations about gender roles and household tasks, and consider if you want to change any of your expectations that no longer have a positive influence on your life. Many of the gender-role stereotypes that abound in society simply are not true. These stereotypes, however, can influence partners in relationships to take on roles that either are not healthy for them (as in the case of a woman becoming submissive to her husband to the extent that she is abused by him) or that limit their ability to participate fully in their relationships (such as a man who fears expressing his emotions to his partner because he has learned that's not what "a real man" is supposed to do).

A social debate surrounds the question of whether "traditional" marriages (in which the wife stays home and cares for the children and the home, and the husband is the breadwinner focused on building his career) or "egalitarian" marriages (in which both partners share equal responsibility for caring for all household tasks) are more beneficial for spouses, children, and the general structure of society. However, satisfying marital relationships can occur within traditional and egalitarian relationships—depending on the partners' preferences. Also, couples may create a variety of other types of marriages that fall somewhere in between a traditional or egalitarian marriage— such as a marriage in which the father stays home and assumes most of the household responsibilities or a marriage in which partners share some of the household responsibilities, but one partner may contribute more in certain other areas. You can probably imagine the tensions that would arise for a couple in which one partner desires a traditional marriage and the other partner desires an egalitarian marriage! As long as partners can agree on the type of marriage they both desire, they're likely to be able to work out a relational context that is satisfying to both partners.

Because of the influence that gender role expectations have on marriage, examine your expectations surrounding gender, as well as the influences on these expectations. Gender affects men's and women's socialization and development. Many influences have shaped your attitudes and beliefs about gender roles and household tasks. Notably, the division of labor in your family-of-origin and stereotypes in the media and surrounding culture powerfully impact your attitudes. These influences shape the expectations you have about your marriage. Complete the following exercise to examine the lessons you learned about the division of household tasks from your family-of-origin and the media, along with your expectations for your marriage.

Directions: Who did each of these tasks in your family-of-origin? Which gender is likely to do each task in the media (e.g., movies and television)? Finally, who will do each task in your marriage?

Use the following codes to represent the gender that held primary responsibility for each task:

F = A female

M = A male

B = Both

Discuss the similarities and differences between your and your partner's responses.

PARTNER A	PARTNER B

▶ **Paying bills**

In your family:

_____   _____

In the media:

_____   _____

In your marriage:

_____   _____

PARTNER A	PARTNER B

▶ **Fixing things around the house**

In your family:

_____   _____

In the media:

_____   _____

In your marriage:

_____   _____

▶ **Doing laundry**

In your family:

_____   _____

In the media:

_____   _____

In your marriage:

_____   _____

▶ **Cleaning**

In your family:

_____   _____

In the media:

_____   _____

In your marriage:

_____   _____

CONTINUED

PARTNER A	PARTNER B

▶ **Shopping for groceries**

In your family:

_____   _____

In the media:

_____   _____

In your marriage:

_____   _____

▶ **Cooking dinner**

In your family:

_____   _____

In the media:

_____   _____

In your marriage:

_____   _____

▶ **Taking care of pets**

In your family:

_____   _____

In the media:

_____   _____

In your marriage:

_____   _____

PARTNER A	PARTNER B

▶ **Taking children to appointments**

In your family:

_____   _____

In the media:

_____   _____

In your marriage:

_____   _____

▶ **Disciplining children**

In your family:

_____   _____

In the media:

_____   _____

In your marriage:

_____   _____

▶ **Mowing the lawn**

In your family:

_____   _____

In the media:

_____   _____

In your marriage:

_____   _____

Who Will Do What, When?

The issue of dividing household labor is more complicated than it first seems. Even when you agree on the tasks each partner will complete, your arrangements will probably not work in all situations. For example, many couples strive to divide the housework fifty-fifty, with each partner sharing equal responsibilities. Good luck if you strive for such an arrangement! Complete equality is nearly impossible, as an objective standard does not exist to rate the value of each task. Is doing the laundry equal to cleaning the toilets? Is vacuuming the carpet equivalent to scrubbing the bathtub? I suspect that all of us have own ideas about the amount of work required for each task.

Further complicating the division of household labor are cultural norms that suggest that women are more responsible than men for the maintenance of the household. Many women feel pressure to oversee household tasks, even when their husbands participate and/or the couple has outside help. In fact, research suggests that women shoulder most household responsibilities, even in egalitarian relationships and when both partners have careers. Women who work outside the home still tend to do most of the housework. This trend is known as *the second shift*, in which career women come home after work only to face more work in the household.

Keeping score as to who has done what in the household sends a couple on a path to resentment, disappointment, and conflict. Trust me on this one. I *hate* to clean, so dividing the housework evenly with my husband was one of my biggest concerns when I first married. I was determined that my relationship would defy the standard. My husband and I discussed the biggest routine cleaning tasks, and we identified "the big four": vacuuming, mopping, cleaning the toilets and tub, and dusting. We each selected our least-hated tasks from that list and agreed to perform those tasks regularly. We also established general guidelines for the housework. For example, the person who cooks dinner does not wash dishes, and each person does his or her laundry separately.

For the most part, these arrangements worked well. At times, however, I noticed that my husband left trash in the living room, or he did not take out the trash as often as I did, or he left dirty dishes in the sink. I began to see these acts as a pattern, and I became very angry with my husband. Over time, I realized that although we share responsibilities, I sometimes do more than my share of the work. Likewise, there are times when he picks up the slack for me. Still, I dream of the day that we can easily afford to hire a cleaning service!

Figure out the best arrangement for your marriage—and keep in mind that these arrangements will probably change over time. Couples make many types of arrangements that can lead to a satisfying division of labor—try to determine which arrangement would work best for your marriage. Some couples strive to share all tasks—cooking together, cleaning together, running errands together, and so on. Other couples clearly define the tasks that are each partner's responsibility. Still other couples take care of tasks as they arise, maintaining flexibility in their arrangements. Consider the following questions as you develop an arrangement for your marriage:

- Which tasks does each partner not mind doing?

- Which tasks does each partner despise?

- How often will cleaning be done?

- What expectations do you have about the type of household you desire (i.e., the level of cleanliness of your house and the types of meals you like to eat)?

- How much time does each partner have to devote to caring for the home, given work responsibilities and other obligations?

- Can you afford to hire outside help to assist you with the household responsibilities (e.g., a cleaning service, a landscaper, or a grocery delivery service)?

No easy solutions exist for dividing up the household work. It will take some trial and error to discover what works best. Discuss your arrangement on a regular basis with your partner. Don't allow resentment and anger to grow if you are dissatisfied with the division of labor. Express your concerns, and brainstorm solutions to problems that arise.

How Will It Be Done?

As you read in the case study about Simone and Greg at the beginning of this chapter, married partners often hold different expectations for their home. Some people prefer an immaculate, clean home, while others are content with a little disorder. Some people like to eat fancy meals for dinner each night, while other people are satisfied with a frozen pizza and a can of soda. Spouses are fortunate when they share the same values for their home. For many couples, however, each partner's expectations differ slightly or vastly. Different expectations can lead to big disagreements. In this section, I discuss strategies for carrying out household responsibilities, including letting go of perfection and maintaining flexibility in your arrangements.

Let Go of Perfection

Consider the differences in your and your partner's standards for the household. How compatible are your expectations? Hopefully, your and your partner's standards are similar. If, however, you prefer a higher standard of household cleanliness than your partner, you may need to lower your standards for the sake of peace in the marriage. You do not need to allow your home to become a complete mess, but you may need to release your desire to maintain a "perfect" home. Sometimes, it's okay to leave the dishes in the sink and wash them later. It is okay to have mismatched pillows or to not have the table set perfectly for every meal. Domestic perfection is an admirable goal; however, it is rarely possible to accomplish, especially if you have other obligations—such as children, work, or a social life.

Learn how to delegate tasks to your partner. If you want your partner to do something, let your partner do it his or her way! Show your partner how you prefer to complete the task, but accept that your partner may prefer another method. As long as the job gets done, be happy you did not have to do it yourself. You waste time if you stand over your partner's shoulder to ensure that the task is done "right" or if you go back to correct an inept job. In either case, you were better off doing the task yourself from the start. The bottom line is this: If you ask someone to do something, be flexible. If you are not comfortable with the result, do it yourself.

Being less concerned than your partner with the condition of your household is not an excuse to get out of sharing in the household responsibilities. Make compromises and work harder than you might on your own. If you do not share household responsibilities, your partner may resent you, particularly if you create more work. Your spouse is your *partner*, not your housekeeper or employee. Share the household tasks as you share in the joy of having a nice home.

Maintain Flexibility in the Household

Even if you are both satisfied with your plans for sharing household responsibilities, situations will arise that challenge your arrangements. As your relationship grows and changes, the division of labor will change as well. Over time, you will experience changes that alter the responsibilities of maintaining your home—such as moving to a larger house, changing careers, or having a baby. These and other changes (e.g., a new work schedule or different seasons of the year) impact the division of labor.

A significant change you may face that will alter household responsibilities is the birth of a child. If one or both of you already has children when you marry, you will face this issue immediately. If you do not yet have children, the arrangements that work well for you as a childless couple may not work once you become parents. Couples with children are especially likely to disagree about the division of household labor. Significant gender role expectations surround parenting, and gender equality is often impossible within the context of parenting. Children create more cleaning, laundry, cooking, and dirty dishes. Previously manageable responsibilities can become overwhelming to new parents, so old arrangements need to change to meet new demands.

Any change brings the possibility of a need to modify your division of household labor. Maintain flexibility in your plans. Challenge your expectations and plans as new experiences arise. Be willing to take on new responsibilities and leave others behind as your needs change. Most important, communicate with your partner and support each other through these changes.

Conclusion

Married couples often disagree about how to maintain the household. If this is a struggle in your relationship, you are not alone! Develop strategies to manage your household and share the responsibilities. Consider the influence of your gender role expectations on your desires for your household. Examine those expectations, and change them if necessary. Throughout your marriage, maintain an open conversation with your spouse about the question, "Who will do what, when, and how?" This is not an easy question to answer. As you strive to answer it, you have opportunities to deepen and strengthen your relationship.

Action Plan: Gender Role Expectations and Household Tasks

1. Evaluate the expectations you hold related to gender and household tasks within marriage.

2. Discuss with your partner how you will divide the tasks required to maintain your household once you are married.

3. Agree upon the standards to which you will aspire regarding your household tasks (e.g., timing and level of cleanliness).

4. Maintain flexibility in your household arrangements to account for new circumstances over time.

Discussion Questions

1. How were household responsibilities divided in your family-of-origin?

2. How much do you enjoy various household tasks? What is your favorite thing to do? What is your least favorite thing to do?

3. What would be the ideal arrangement for you and your future spouse to use to divide the housework?

4. Do you have expectations about tasks that are more appropriate for men or for women to do? How could these expectations influence your marriage?

5. What would do if you felt that your partner was not doing a fair share of the household tasks?

6. How would you like your partner to approach you if she felt that way about you?

One day, Pauline visited the apartment of her fiancé, Andre. While checking her e-mail on his computer, she noticed a credit card bill on his desk. She noticed that the debt on the credit card was more than $7,000. She was shocked! Pauline thought Andre was very conservative with money, and she had no idea he had so much debt. She wondered if she would be responsible for that debt once they married and if Andre had any other debt she didn't know about.

When Pauline asked Andre about his debt and why he hadn't told her about it previously, he responded, "I'm taking care of it. I didn't think it was important for you to know about because I'm handling it on my own, and I didn't want to worry you."

Pauline was upset by Andre's response, but she wasn't sure how to respond. So, she just dropped the topic and decided she'd try to talk to him about it more later.

thirteen
Finances

The discovery of Andre's credit card debt concerned Pauline about their financial future. Many financial issues affect marriage: debt, spending habits, financial goals, financial decision-making, differing incomes, and legal responsibilities. Upon marriage, couples may choose to combine their finances completely, maintain totally separate finances, or use some combination of shared and individual money. In each case, couples face many financial decisions that can influence their relationship, as these issues introduce possible sources of conflict into marital relationships. In fact, money is one of the most common causes of disagreements for newly married couples.

This chapter reviews some financial issues you may face as you prepare to marry. The focus of this chapter is not on providing specific financial advice; you will find a list of additional resources for that information at the end of the chapter. Rather, this chapter addresses the relational aspects of finances as they impact engaged and newly married couples. I first discuss the decision to have a prenuptial agreement, which can create stress in even the strongest relationship. I then review issues related to combining your finances, and I include an exercise that examines the compatibility of your spending habits. Finally, I discuss the importance of shared financial goals.

Prenuptial Agreements: For Love or Money?

The decision to have a prenuptial agreement presents a struggle between one's mind and heart. The logical mind thinks it wise to have a prenuptial agreement in case the relationship doesn't last. After all, the mind reasons, "More than half of marriages today end in divorce. It is possible that my marriage won't work out, isn't it?"

"Not so fast," warns the passionate heart. "Our marriage will be different. I don't want to entertain the thought that this marriage won't last. And I certainly do not want my partner to think I have doubts."

There are some situations in which a prenuptial agreement may not be necessary—such as when both partners have virtually no personal assets. In other situations, most financial planners, including Suze Orman, author of *The Road to Wealth: A Comprehensive Guide to Your Money*, believe that a having prenuptial agreement is a good idea. It is not pleasant to think about divorce during your engagement. However, a prenuptial agreement provides you with security and peace of mind, knowing you have some degree of protection if a divorce occurs, even if there is a million-to-one chance of that happening. You also offer the same security to your beloved spouse-to-be. For many couples, a prenuptial agreement is something that is better to have and never use than to not have when it is highly needed.

A prenuptial agreement helps you avoid an ugly, emotionally distressing battle if you divorce. I have witnessed divorce mediation and was struck by the nastiness of the attacks between the partners as they attempted to divide their assets and arrange child custody agreements. While I observed the divorce mediation in progress, I thought to myself that even these partners—despite all of their nastiness and resentment toward each other—certainly were loving and caring toward each other at one time. Many of their points of conflict could have been averted through a prenuptial agreement, but many couples do not consider such protection before they marry.

The issues you might cover in a prenuptial agreement include protection of assets held prior to marriage, future stock holdings, retirement accounts, and debt. Speak with a lawyer in your state to determine the specific provisions that are allowable. In most situations, you and your partner should have your own attorneys to help you through the process. Select your attorney carefully. Find an attorney who will look out for your best interest while remaining respectful of your spouse and relationship. Avoid attorneys who display the following warning signs: cynicism about marriage, failing to listen carefully to your needs and requests, and a combative attitude toward your partner and his or her attorney. Everyone must cooperate to arrange the best possible agreement for you, your future spouse, and your marriage.

Broaching the Topic of Prenuptial Agreements

Beyond the specifics of prenuptial agreements, the more relevant issue for this book is how to talk about this issue with your partner without causing a major rift in your relationship. First, talk with your partner about a prenuptial agreement, as with all other financial matters, as soon as you can. The sooner you discuss a prenuptial agreement, the longer you have to make arrangements in a calm, understanding manner. Second, if your partner requests a prenuptial agreement of you, understand his or her reasons for doing so. Perhaps his parents had a bitter divorce in which one parent was left with nothing. Perhaps a former boyfriend of hers scammed her for money. Your partner is probably thinking more about personal security than doubting your intentions or the future sustainability of your marriage. Finally, if you request the prenuptial agreement and your partner disagrees, be respectful but firm. You have a right to protect your future well-being. If she still refuses to sign the prenuptial agreement, then you will need to consider whether you want to enter into a marriage with someone who is unwilling to compromise on this issue.

Marital Finances: To Combine or Not to Combine

Combining finances following marriage can be a smooth transition or a difficult struggle. Marital finances involve more than simply getting your paychecks, depositing them in the same bank account, and then paying all of your bills together. Along with shared finances come complicating factors—such as unequal incomes, pre-existing debt, differing spending habits, unique financial goals and needs, and major purchases (e.g., a new home or car).

There are about as many different financial arrangements as there are married couples. For example, some couples combine all their money into one pool and share all decisions jointly. Some couples keep incomes totally separate and divide the shared expenses. Still others combine some money, but each partner also maintains an individual account with a fixed amount or percentage of his or her income. There is no one right way to guarantee financial happiness. Discuss with your partner which option is best for you. In so doing, consider the following issues: your personal spending habits, financial decision-making, and your attitudes toward debt.

Spending Habits
Consider the following three situations:

- One partner clips coupons out of the Sunday paper every week and shops at discount stores. The other partner likes to buy top-of-the-line merchandise, regardless of the cost.

- A couple is in the market for a car. One partner only wants to look at new cars, because of the long-term warranties available and because, "You never know who had a used car before you or how they treated the car." The other partner wants to buy a used car, saying, "It's ridiculous to buy a new car and let it depreciate as soon as you drive off the lot."

- Another couple is buying a new washer and dryer. One partner is interested in the machines that were rated highest by a leading consumer magazine. However, the other partner is more interested in finding machines that "feel right" and look good in the basement.

Each couple is experiencing a common situation for newlyweds. Even if you and your partner agree on most financial matters, you probably hold different attitudes toward spending money in certain areas (such as entertainment, gifts, or travel). For example, you may agree about the types of cars you drive, but you disagree about how much to spend weekly on groceries. Complete the following exercise to examine the differences and similarities in your spending habits.

Directions: In the spaces provided, write how much you think you and your partner should spend *per month* on each category. Complete the exercise separately, and compare your answers. Notice the similarities and differences between your spending plans. Discuss any major differences, and consider how you might compromise.

PARTNER A	PARTNER B

▶ Rent/mortgage

$ _____ $ _____

▶ Food/groceries

$ _____ $ _____

▶ Clothing

$ _____ $ _____

▶ Car payment, gas, and repairs

$ _____ $ _____

▶ Dining out

$ _____ $ _____

▶ Other entertainment

$ _____ $ _____

PARTNER A	PARTNER B

► Personal care (haircuts, manicures, etc.)

$ _____ $ _____

► Taxes

$ _____ $ _____

► Charity and religious contributions

$ _____ $ _____

► Savings

$ _____ $ _____

► Education or career-related expenses

$ _____ $ _____

► Individual discretionary money

$ _____ $ _____

► Travel

$ _____ $ _____

► Miscellaneous

$ _____ $ _____

After completing this exercise, you will have an idea about the spending areas in which you and your partner hold different viewpoints. Fortunately, you and your partner can live in financial peace despite your differences. The keys to peace are *compromise* and *negotiation*. In finances, like most other areas, you can't expect to get your way all the time. Nor should you expect your own preferences to be ignored all of the time. Rather, expect that you will get your way some of the time and your partner will get his or her way some of the time, but most of the time you will meet in the middle.

Compromise on financial issues whenever you can. The couples in the situations at the start of this section can resolve their differences through compromise. The couple in the first situation could decide that the big-spending partner will buy the top brands only when the coupon-clipping partner can find the products on sale. The second couple may decide to buy a one-year-old car, which is still under warranty, from someone they know and trust. The third couple could buy a washer and a dryer that looks good and "feels right" and that is also ranked highly by the consumer magazine. The most effective way to discover solutions is to consider how financial decisions will be made.

Financial Decision-Making: His, Hers, or Theirs?

Who will make which financial decisions in your marriage? Will they be shared equally? Will each partner be responsible for certain decisions? What will you do when your partner is unavailable and a decision must be made?

These are not easy decisions. An arrangement to share equally all financial decisions may be impractical. For example, it is not an effective use of time for both partners to pay all of the monthly bills together if one partner could complete the same task in the same amount of time with equal efficiency. On the other hand, an arrangement for only one partner to make all of the financial decisions may lead the other partner to feel ignored, disrespected, and unaware of their financial situation. Discover the best way to set up your financial decision-making in your marriage, and know that your arrangements will change over time as your needs change. Consider how you and your partner will share responsibility for making financial decisions. Together with your partner, answer the following questions.

Who wants to be responsible for the family's finances? Although it is best if both of you are involved, one partner may be more interested in or knowledgeable about finances and wish to take on more responsibility. Even if one partner chooses to be less involved, ensure that both partners remain knowledgeable about your family's financial situation.

Who has time to devote to the family finances? Maintaining financial health takes a sizable time commitment. Individuals and families with the healthiest financial situations devote time and energy to matters of money. Whoever takes primary responsibility for the family's finances must commit the necessary time and energy to maintain a positive financial outlook.

Which decisions require joint discussion? In some situations, a shared decision is not possible immediately. For example, one of your cars breaks down and is taken to the auto shop for emergency repairs, and you need to decide immediately how much to spend on the repairs. It is not pragmatic to share every decision—such as how much to spend on laundry detergent or which brand of bread to buy. Partners must trust one another to make financial decisions in situations in which it is neither possible nor pragmatic to discuss the issue together. Discuss with your partner the types of decisions you will make together and individually. It may be helpful to set a particular dollar amount for purchases, above which partners must consult each other prior to making a purchase. This dollar amount for couples on a tight budget might be $50, while it may be $300 for couples with a larger amount of disposable income.

How will you learn more about money management to enhance your financial decisions? Identify resources to help you to make sound financial decisions. The books in the "Conclusion and Additional Resources" section at the end of this chapter are a good starting point. Other resources include a trusted financial advisor, television programs, radio shows, magazines, and newspapers. Be cautious in deciding which information to use, as a lot of misinformation is out there. As you become more knowledgeable about financial matters, you will become better equipped to secure a prosperous financial future.

Exploring Your Attitudes Toward Debt

What is your attitude toward debt? Do you want to avoid it at all costs and pay off loans as soon as possible? Or do you believe debt is a normal part of life, and you don't worry about how long it takes to pay off? Read the following statements, and rate them 1 to 10 based on your attitudes toward debt, with 1 being "strongly agree," 5 representing "neutral," and 10 representing "strongly disagree." Ask your partner to do the same.

- I fear debt.

- I don't mind debt.

- I am paralyzed by the thought of carrying a lot of debt.

- Having debt allows me to have things I want now and pay later.

How close are your and your partner's assessments? Whether you share the same beliefs or are on opposite ends of the extremes, discuss debt with your partner before you marry. This conversation could prevent trouble later, because you may be held responsible for any debt that your partner accrues during your marriage, even if she does so without your knowledge or approval. If you prefer to pay off your credit cards every month but your partner enjoys maxing out all of his or her credit cards and making minimum monthly payments, you could be headed for financial ruin.

Don't assume that your partner's attitudes toward debt are the same as yours. Several years ago, while my husband and I were enjoying lunch with a friend and her boyfriend of about one year, the topic of debt came up, and one of the partners said something to the tune of, "I'll always have debt, and I'm fine with that. I'd rather enjoy what I can now." That revelation shocked the other partner. Apparently, they had never had that conversation before! Before you and your partner assume the legal rights and responsibilities accorded to married couples, talk about debt. Have this conversation now to avoid some disappointing surprises later on.

Developing Shared Financial Goals

This chapter ends on a positive note. If you and your partner communicate openly about your finances, you can achieve your financial goals, assuming they are realistic and you work to make them happen. Marriage offers many financial benefits. Therefore, you may be in a better position to achieve your financial goals when you are married. Consider your personal financial goals and the manner in which these will shape your shared goals. Having financial goals helps you make financial decisions. When a dilemma arises, you can examine the possible solutions in light of your goals. Ask yourselves, "Which decision will bring us closer to our goals?" Prioritize your financial decisions in relation to these goals. Re-evaluate your goals often, as your life circumstances and financial resources will change. Long-term financial wealth takes time, sacrifice, and compromise in the short-term. Work with your partner toward your individual and shared goals, and create a prosperous future. Complete the following exercise to outline your personal and shared financial goals.

Directions: Write your top three to five personal financial goals in the spaces provided. Ask your partner to do the same.

PARTNER A'S GOALS

_____

_____

_____

_____

_____

_____

PARTNER B'S GOALS

_____

_____

_____

_____

_____

_____

Circle any goals that are similar or identical to your partner. Rewrite them in the following list of shared goals. Discuss any other goals you would like to work toward together. Add those additional goals to the list.

SHARED GOALS

1. _____

2. _____

3. _____

4. _____

5. _____

6. _____

7. _____

8. _____

9. _____

Finally, go back through your shared goals to see if they seem to be realistic, given your current financial situation, your career choices, and other relevant information. Replace any goals that are not realistic with attainable objectives.

Conclusion and Additional Resources

Financial planning causes stress for many newly married couples. Prepare for some of the financial issues that may arise as you become married—such as deciding on a prenuptial agreement, combining your finances, and making financial decisions. Careful consideration of these issues prepares you to share your life, and your money, with your future spouse.

Many financial books are available that are packed with specific financial guidance to assist couples. Some books you may find helpful include the following:

Bach, David. *Smart Couples Finish Rich: Nine Steps to Creating a Rich Future for You and Your Partner* (New York: Broadway Books, 2001).

Kimball, Cheryl, and Faye Kathryn Doria, CFP. *The Everything Get Out of Debt Book: Evaluate Your Options, Determine Your Course of Action, and Make a Fresh Start* (Avon, MA: Adams Media, 2002).

Orman, Suze. *The Road to Wealth: A Comprehensive Guide to Your Money* (New York: Riverhead Books, 2001).

Schwab-Pomerantz, Carrie, and Charles Schwab. *It Pays to Talk: How to Have the Essential Conversations with Your Family about Money and Investing* (New York: Three Rivers Press, 2002).

Stanley, Thomas J., and William D. Danko. *The Millionaire Next Door: The Surprising Secrets of America's Wealthy* (Atlanta, GA: Longstreet Press, 1999).

Action Plan: Finances

1. Decide whether a prenuptial agreement is right for you and your relationship.

2. Evaluate the advantages and disadvantages of combining your finances with your partner.

3. Compare your spending habits to identify your similarities and differences.

4. Develop shared financial goals.

5. Seek out additional resources for financial information to help your marriage start with a solid financial foundation.

Discussion Questions

1. What are your personal financial goals? Be as specific as you can.

2. What kind of lifestyle do you desire? How much money will it take to have that lifestyle?

3. What kind of spender are you (conservative, lavish, impulsive, etc.)? Where did you learn these spending habits?

4. How much of a role would you like to have in the financial decision-making within your marriage?

5. Which financial decisions should always be made together? Which decisions can one partner make without consulting the other person?

Joanna and Ken, who recently became engaged, come from very different family backgrounds. Joanna's family is close and communicative, and they spend a lot of time together. Joanna's parents have been married for almost thirty years, and she has two older brothers with whom she gets along well.

In contrast, the relationships in Ken's family are distant and ridden with conflict. Although Ken lives only two hours away from his family, he sees them only once every few years. His parents divorced when he was ten, and he has had a difficult time relating to both of them ever since that time. He also has a strained relationship with his only sibling, a younger sister. He made efforts to reconcile with his parents and sister, but they never seem to be able to get past their differences.

As they prepare to get married, Joanna and Ken wonder how their family relationships will influence their marriage. Ken gets along well with Joanna's family, but Joanna has only met Ken's family members one time. The couple hopes to have a happy marriage in which they are close to both partner's families.

fourteen
Family-of-Origin Issues

One of the most powerful influences on your marriage is your family background. You are not destined to have the same kind of marriage your parents had—for better or worse—but the family environment in which you were raised shaped who you are today. Joanna and Ken are similar to many engaged couples that reflect upon the type of influences their family backgrounds are likely to have on their future marriage. In this chapter, we consider a number of family-related issues, including the transmission of marital patterns across generations, strategies to enhance relationships with your families, and steps to build healthy relationships with your in-laws.

The Transmission of Marital Patterns Across Generations

The characteristics of your family-of-origin have a powerful influence on the course of your marriage. Patterns within parents' marriages are often replayed in the marriages of their children—although you are not destined to re-create the same dynamics that were present in your parents' relationships. Reflecting on the relationships within your family-of-origin helps you enter marriage with awareness of how these patterns could play out in your marriage—as well as those patterns that you would like to change. Complete the following exercise to examine the relationships in your families-of-origin.

Directions: To the best of your knowledge, describe each of the following relationships in three words. Ask your partner to do the same. Then discuss the questions at the end of the exercise.

PARTNER A	PARTNER B

▶ Your parents' marriage/relationship

_____   _____

_____   _____

_____   _____

▶ Your maternal grandparents' marriage

_____   _____

_____   _____

_____   _____

▶ Your paternal grandparents' marriage

_____   _____

_____   _____

_____   _____

▶ Your relationships with your siblings

_____   _____

_____   _____

_____   _____

▶ Other influential relationships in your life (e.g., step-parents, step-siblings, siblings' marriages)

_____   _____

_____   _____

_____   _____

Discussion Questions

1. What patterns do you notice in these relationships?

2. What differences do you see between your and your partner's responses?

3. What similarities do you see between your and your partner's responses?

Marriage patterns can be positive or negative. For example, some couples strive to create a marriage that is similar to their parents' marriages, which include open communication, honesty, respect, and deep love. Many couples learn positive relationship skills from their families-of-origin by observing their parents' marriages and having positive relationships with family members. For example, *The Changing Family Life Cycle: A Framework for Family Therapy*, edited by Betty Carter and Monica McGoldrick, reports that sibling relationships often serve as models for marital relationships. When relationships are positive, people carry constructive relationship patterns into their romantic relationships.

Sometimes, negative patterns within families are replayed in offspring's marriages. Two patterns that can be transmitted across generations are divorce and poor marital quality. A number of research studies have shown that parental divorce is a risk factor for marital distress. As Paul Amato and Danelle DeBoer note in the *Journal of Marriage and Family*, "Parental divorce is one of the best documented risk factors for marital dissolution." Couples in which one or both partners experienced parental divorce face a greater risk of divorce themselves, and this is particularly true for women, according to a study published in the *Journal of Divorce* by researchers Alan Edwards and John Booth. The existing research doesn't yet explain why women appear to be especially vulnerable to the effects of parental divorce, but it does suggest that women who have experienced the divorce of their parents may want to give careful consideration to that experience as they prepare for marriage. Parental divorce can influence children's marriages through strained parent-child relationships, distant and disorganized family relationships, and the attitudes that adult children of divorced parents hold toward marriage. If you or your partner experienced the divorce of your parents, consider how that experience could influence your marriage.

Overcoming a Legacy of Divorce

As an adult child of divorce myself—who is also married to another adult child of divorce—I was very distressed upon learning the trends I described in the previous paragraph in the early days of my relationship with my husband. Therefore, it is also important to note that individuals who have experienced their parents' divorces may also develop some unique strengths and resources that can help them create positive, satisfying adult intimate relationships. For one thing, individuals who witness parental divorces often have a powerful model of "what not to do" in marriage. As such, they could become more likely to identify early warning signs to alert them of potential trouble within their own marriages. In addition, the past experience of parental divorce can provide an additional source of motivation to work on making one's own marriage more resistant to divorce.

The quality of your parents' marriages can actually have a more powerful influence on the course of your future marriage than whether or not your parents are divorced. Couples may experience less commitment to marriage, marital instability, and more disagreements when one or both of their parents had unhappy marriages. Couples may also be more likely to remain in unhappy marriages if their parents did so. When children observe their parents being unhappy, abusive, mistreated, unfaithful, or angry within their intimate relationships, it makes sense that they might grow to be skeptical of close relationships and their own intimate partners as adults. Likewise, positive relationship qualities—such as supportive communication, displays of affection, and effective strategies for conflict management—in parents' relationships help children learn that intimate relationships can be nurturing and loving.

Your marriage occurs within the context of your and your partner's experiences within your families. Many people marry partners who come from families with similar relationship patterns. Some people strive to create a marriage that is entirely different from the marriages of their parents. Consider a person whose family has intensely close relationships, which feel smothering. This person is likely to seek a spouse who agrees to more independence in the marriage. Your family had a powerful force in shaping who you are, and you cannot separate yourself entirely from the patterns that played out in your family-of-origin. Your marriage will be similar in some ways to your family relationships, yet it will also be different.

You are not destined to repeat the past in your marriage. Increase the likelihood that you will chart your own life course by gaining awareness of the relational patterns in your family-of-origin. Work actively to change the less adaptive patterns in your marriage. Examine the relationships in your families while you are engaged, and decide which aspects of your family relationships you wish to maintain and those that you wish to change.

Enhancing Your Relationships with Your Own Family-of-Origin

As the previous sections of this chapter demonstrate, your extended family relationships can have a powerful influence on your upcoming marriage. Enhance your family relationships to create a more positive context for your marriage. Your family can provide you with social support. When your family supports you and your marriage, your marriage can flourish and grow. Whenever possible, strengthen your bonds within your families to create strong relationships within each partner's family.

One challenge that families face following a new marriage is renegotiating the roles within the family. Successful marital adjustment involves navigating your relationships with your family in light of your new marriage. Your new family with your spouse is separate from, yet influenced by, your family-of-origin. In the past, you may have turned to your parents for advice and support. However, now you consult your spouse first. You may feel a distance between you and your parents, and your parents may feel that they are less important to you. Renegotiating these roles and adjusting your family relationships takes time, and it can be more complicated because you'll also be experiencing changes in your roles in your relationship with your partner at the same time. You will probably begin to relate to your parents in a friendship relationship, more than as a parent-child relationship. Prepare for some possible struggles along the way. The following strategies may help you to negotiate these roles and strengthen your family relationships.

Tell Your Family Members What You Want from Your Relationships

If you desire a closer relationship with your father, tell him. If you wish that you and your mother could spend more time together, tell her. If you would like to resolve long-standing conflicts with your siblings, tell them. Your family members cannot read your mind and know what you want if you do not tell them. They may not recognize subtle clues or unclear attempts to strengthen your relationships. Your family members may not have the time, energy, or desire to create the same type of relationship with you that you desire, or they may want the same type of relationship you desire, but they are too afraid to ask.

Speak directly about your desires with your family members so you can work toward shared goals. Even if family members are not willing to work on your relationships with them at this time, you can leave the door open for a closer connection in the future.

Address Family Members' Concerns about Your Upcoming Marriage

If your parents or other family members do not approve of your marriage, many problems can develop in your relationship. Discuss these concerns directly with your family members so you can understand the source of their concerns. Decide if their concerns are legitimate or unfounded. Perhaps they know something that you're not willing to see. Or, perhaps you know a side of your partner that your family members have not yet had the opportunity to observe. Understand their concerns, describe your position, and work to resolve your differences together. These concerns will not go away automatically once you get married. Listen to them openly, and address the concerns now to prevent bigger differences later.

Focus On What *You* Can Do

The best way to change your relationships with your family members is to change yourself in relation to them. A long, often ineffective, struggle arises when you try to convince someone else to change. For example, you might not succeed in convincing your mother to stop making insensitive comments to you about your future spouse. It is easier and more effective for you to change *your* behavior in response to the other person. If your mother makes an insensitive comment to you, change your behavior from ignoring her comments to telling her how the comments hurt you, and then ending the conversation if she continues. You can always change your own behavior more easily than you can change someone else's behavior. Consider the changes you can make to enhance your relationships with your family members.

Spend Time Alone with Your Family Members

Get to know your family members more closely. Create time for your family members so you will have a foundation for building a stronger relationship. Begin with just one person, preferably the person who is most motivated and available to work on your relationship, and then build on other relationships later. Share the details of your lives with one another. It might be helpful to keep up with traditions even after you are married, such as going shopping with your mother once a month or still visiting your parents for weekly Sunday dinners. You may have to work to create time for your relationships, especially if you live far away. If your family relationships cross the miles, set up regular times for visits and phone conversations in order to stay involved in one another's lives. Ultimately, the time you spend will help you build more supportive, closer relationships.

Encourage Your Partner to Spend Time with Your Family

Once you are married, it will be difficult for you to be close with your family members if they do not get along with your spouse. Your spouse is your new family, so work on joining your new family with your family-of-origin. Encourage your partner to develop personal relationships and shared experiences with your family members. In so doing, you strengthen your own connections with your family. One way to start is to have each spouse send the thank-you notes for wedding gifts to the other spouse's family members. Although this strategy might lead to some anxiety for both partners, it can be a nice way to demonstrate your openness to building relationships with your new in-laws.

Write Letters to Communicate Effectively

Some people communicate more effectively through the written word. Some people find it difficult to express all of their ideas during a spoken conversation. Your wedding is a sentimental and momentous occasion for all of your family members. You may experience deep appreciation and love for your family members for their support in getting to this moment in your life. Write letters to your family members to express your gratitude. These letters often become important keepsakes that preserve your family relationships and history.

In-Laws

Establish strong bonds with your new in-laws as you prepare for marriage. This transition is not always easy. Struggles with in-laws are a normal part of the developmental processes within marriage. In-law relationships can be incredibly supportive. They are also often notoriously wrought with conflict—although many stereotypical depictions of in-laws are highly exaggerated. Expect some normal in-law tension as you enter marriage. Some couples even use conflicts with in-laws as outlets for tensions within their marriages. Resolving the normal tensions that surrounds in-law relationships strengthens your marriage. Take the following steps to improve your relationships with your in-laws.

Encourage Your Partner to Work on the Relationships Within His or Her Family

In-law relationships are especially difficult when each partner is not close with his or her family members. Conflicts or tensions between family members are often projected on to the spouse, which prevents the new spouse from developing strong relationships with the in-laws. When each partner enhances the relationships in his or her family, in-law relationships improve more easily. Encourage your partner to improve those family relationships, and help your partner determine the best strategies to enhance those relationships.

Spend Time Alone with Your Partner's Family Members

Establish one-on-one relationships with the members of your partner's family. Let them get to know you individually, and not just as the partner of their child, grandchild, or sibling. Also, learn more about each of your future in-laws. The more you know about each other, the easier it will be to diffuse tension. You may find that a single lunch out with your soon-to-be mother-in-law goes a long way toward enhancing your relationship with her.

Encourage Your Partner to Spend Time Alone with His or Her Family

Some of your partner's family members will probably continue to wish for time alone with your partner after you are married. This is especially true for family members who were close before the marriage. Remember: this desire has nothing to do with the degree to which these family members like you. This desire simply reflects a wish to maintain a close, individual relationship with your partner. Therefore, during visits with your partner's family, offer to spend some time by yourself or with other family members in order to give your partner time alone with his or her family members. By making this offer, you are letting your new in-laws know that you value the relationships they have with your partner.

Involve Your In-Laws in the Wedding Plans

Weddings are ceremonial rituals that establish the new marriage within each partner's family. Enlist the support and talents of your future in-laws. Even if one partner's family is more involved in the wedding plans because of financial reasons, encourage both sides to share in creating a special event for everyone.

Be Open to Different Family Traditions

Tensions arise when family members perceive threats to their family customs. Most families share traditions, stories, and memories that preserve the family bond. Married partners may find that their family's traditions differ. Allow some of each family's traditions to continue within your new marriage.

Be Creative When Problems Arise

As you blend two families, problems are bound to arise. Think creatively to resolve these differences. For example, many couples struggle over how and where to spend the holidays, as people often wish to be with their families during holidays. One creative solution involves combining the families' celebrations and starting new, shared holiday traditions. Other solutions to this problem may involve alternating which family you will visit during each holiday or spending part of the holiday with one family and the other part of the holiday with the other family (particularly if both families live close by). Solutions do not always come easily, but creativity helps you discover original solutions to problems that arise within in-law relationships. Refer back to the problem-solving model described in Chapter 10 when you face other unique challenges.

Conclusion

Family relationships can provide support and challenges to new marriages. Examine the patterns in your families to gain awareness of the patterns in your relationships. Work on enhancing your relationships within your own families, as well as with your future in-laws. Establish close relationships within your families to create a support system that will sustain your marriage for years to come.

Action Plan: Family-of-Origin Issues

1. Recognize that your marriage will be influenced by your parents' relationships, but you are not destined to repeat their relationship patterns—for better or for worse.

2. Use the time while you prepare for marriage to strengthen your relationships with your families whenever possible. Do so by communicating openly with them, focusing on what you can do to change your relationships with them, and including your future spouse in your efforts.

3. Take the time needed to build strong relationships with your future in-laws.

Consider which family traditions you will bring into your marriage from each of your families.

Discussion Questions

1. What qualities of your family-of-origin would you like to re-create in your marriage?

2. In your marriage, what would you like to be different from your family-of-origin?

3. How welcomed do you feel into your partner's family?

4. What problems might arise between you and your new in-laws?

5. What do you think you would do if a conflict arose between your spouse and your parents?

Tré and Sharice married seven months ago. Immediately after their honeymoon, the couple moved to a new city so Sharice could pursue a great career opportunity. Neither Tré nor Sharice knew anyone in this new town before the move, but they were excited to move and start their marriage in a new location.

Upon arriving in their new hometown, both Tré and Sharice became extremely busy in their new jobs, so they had very little time to make friends. They spent all their free time alone with each other. This is very different for them, as they each left a large group of friends behind when they moved to their new location.

Tré and Sharice now feel isolated and lonely living so far from friends and family. Their relationship is strained because neither partner feels that they have anyone to turn to for support during tough times. This has led to some heated arguments, although the couple has always found a way to reconcile once their fights are over.

Tré and Sharice are tired of feeling alone in their new hometown. However, they feel uncertain about how to meet friends because they have such limited time available.

fifteen

Friendships and Social Support

All couples need friends and social contacts for fun, support, and networking. The stress in Tré and Sharice's marriage stems from a lack of such a network. This couple has become very isolated in their new city, which adds pressure to their relationship. Married couples benefit from finding a social network to enhance the growth of their marriages. In this chapter, I discuss the importance of having a social network to support your marriage. We'll discuss the benefits of a supportive social network and see how these support systems increase a couple's chance of having a successful marriage. Finally, I describe how to enhance the social support surrounding your marriage.

The Importance of Social Support

Humans have a basic need for intimacy and connection with others. Although your partner provides some of these things, connections with others provide additional support for you and your relationship. Married couples should seek out connections with social networks. Romantic notions—such as "My partner is everything to me" or "My partner completes me"—exist and suggest that true love fulfills all of a person's needs for intimacy and connection. Despite the romance of these ideas, one person cannot be all things and do all things for you. Having that expectation puts a lot of pressure on your partner and your relationship. Besides, if someone can complete you, then the opposite is also true—she can make you incomplete!

Rather than trying to meet all your needs through your spouse, turn to other people to meet some of your needs. This is where your friends, family, and social support system come in. A strong social support network increases the likelihood that you will have a high-quality, long-lasting marriage. In fact, couples that share mutual friends are less likely to divorce. Also, both men and women are more likely to be satisfied with their marriages when they have supportive social networks. As you prepare for marriage, focus not only on your relationship with your future spouse, but also build connections with a larger support system. Developing a strong social support network can enhance your marriage in many ways, including benefits discussed in this section.

New Opportunities and Experiences

Experience the world around you more fully by connecting with people who have different ideas, connections, and involvements. Friends and acquaintances inform you of exciting social events. You could learn about a job opportunity through an old friend. Your partner may discover a class you would enjoy taking through a coworker. Making connections with other people breathes new life into marriage. You can bring the experiences, information, and personal growth you gain from relationships with other people back to your marriage—providing you and your spouse with interesting topics of conversation, new ideas, and opportunities for your relationship to grow.

The Opportunity to Learn from Others' Mistakes

You will often discover that others have had similar experiences to your own. Marriage may be a new experience for you, but your friends may have already gone through similar marital adjustments. For example, you may feel like you and your partner are the only couple that has experienced disagreements leading up to your wedding. Or perhaps it seems to you that your in-laws treat you worse than any other person's in-laws treat them. However, upon sharing your experiences with members of your support network, you will often discover that your relationship challenges are not unique, and you can learn from how your friends and family members handled those situations. When you learn that a friend has had a similar experience, you'll feel less alone and more normal. Some struggles in marriages are common, and you can learn how other couples succeeded in overcoming these situations. Then consider how the solutions used by others might work in your own marriage.

An Outlet for You to Process Tension in Your Marriage

Isolation breeds resentment and tension—as we saw in the case example of Tré and Sharice at the beginning of this chapter. A social support network provides friends and confidants with whom you can process your experiences in marriage and other areas of your life. This does not mean that you misplace your anger toward your spouse on your friends. Rather, talking with other people helps you consider your situation from a new point of view and provides alternative solutions. Friends offer a fresh perspective on situations in your marriage. People in your social network can be more objective, and they may notice issues you previously could not see. This fresh perspective helps you resolve tension in your marriage.

A Support System Meets the Unique Needs of Each Partner

Your spouse cannot be everything to you, and you cannot be everything to your spouse. For example, imagine that you love to spend time outdoors, and you take a long hike every Saturday morning. Perhaps you do not feel safe hiking alone, but your partner hates to hike. Forcing your partner to be your hiking companion would make your partner unhappy, leading to a less enjoyable hike for you. Finding a new hiking partner allows you to pursue your interest in hiking and your partner to avoid undesirable experiences. You have needs and interests that your partner cannot meet. Of course, most couples expect some basic needs to only be met through their relationships (e.g., the sexual relationship and passionate love). However, a solid social network supports each partner's other individual needs and interests.

Marriage Support

Seek out a social network based on values and beliefs that support your marriage. Simply put, some people encourage you to care for your marital relationship, while other people discourage you from building a stable, satisfying marriage. Surround yourself with people who share your values for marital commitment and stability. Identify people who provide a constant source of positive support for you, your partner, and your marriage. These people will help you build a strong marriage.

Enhancing Support for Your Marriage

Where can you find these supportive people I mentioned in the previous section? And what can you do if you have limited time available for building a social network, as in the case of Tré and Sharice. You can begin to build a social network by considering the support you receive from the people currently involved in your life. Many people probably already support your relationship. You may need to think creatively to identify people you already know who could provide support. For example, Tré and Sharice feel isolated in their new city. However, both partners work, and they may have already met other people through their jobs with whom they could develop friendships. Even if these partners do not foresee any potential friendships with their immediate coworkers, perhaps they make contacts through their work with clients or customers who could become friends over time. Complete the following exercise to examine the current level of social support available to you.

Directions: Each of the circles surrounding "your marriage" in the following diagram represents the support you anticipate you will receive from various components of your social system. Together with your partner, write the names of people or organizations that could support your marriage in the appropriate circle. Examples of sources of support include parents, siblings, extended family members, friends, coworkers, bosses, clients, professional contacts, religious organizations, community organizations, acquaintances, and classmates.

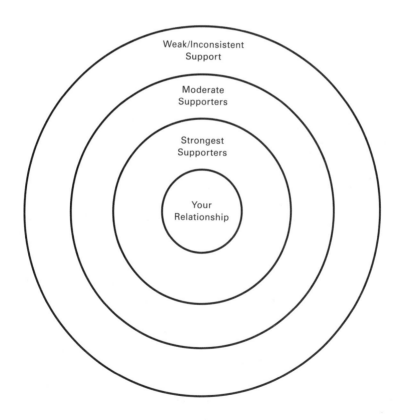

Your social support system will probably change over time as you move through different stages of life. It is likely that your needs for support will change with new life circumstances. For example, a childless couple has no need for friends for "play dates," but this need may become important if the couple eventually has children. All couples at every stage of life can benefit from enhancing their social networks. The following strategies describe ways to build connections with like-minded people.

Reconnect with Old Friends

Re-establish old friendships that slipped away over the years. Perhaps you lost contact with your best friend from high school, but you learn that she is getting married soon, too. Your similar experiences may reconnect you and rebuild your friendship. People often spend less time with friends while dating their future spouses, as they become swept up in the courtship and may neglect friends and other social contacts. If this happened, you may still be able to apologize and reconnect. Old friends provide a great source of social support, as they help you stay true to yourself and remind you of past experiences and memories. You may need to take some risks to contact these old friends out of the blue, but many people would appreciate hearing from an old friend and would welcome the opportunity to reconnect. If a conflict led to the end of your relationship with an old friend, address that issue from the beginning, preferably by offering a sincere apology for your part in the conflict. You and your old friend may still be unable to reconnect, but you can feel satisfied knowing you did your best to try to rectify the situation.

Join a Group with Your Partner

Seek out new connections as a couple to build a jointly constructed support system. Often, couples move between partner's separate social circles. Create a new social circle that is shared equally. A great way to build this type of social network is to join some type of organization together (for example, a local community service organization, a coed sports league through your nearest community center, or a political group that reflects your shared values). Many types of organizations exist, and you can almost certainly find one that reflects your and your partner's shared interests. For example, you may join a club for people who share a similar interest. Many couples also join a religious organization. Find a group that is comfortable for both of you. Joining a group connects you with a community that supports your marriage.

Seek New Experiences

New experiences shared with your partner provide opportunities to meet people who can join your social network. Any number of experiences can introduce you to new people. Take classes in subjects you both enjoy—cooking, dancing, sports, or outdoor adventures. Volunteer at a local nonprofit organization you support. Get out and enjoy cultural events—such as concerts, plays, and lectures—in your community. Join a sports league together. Your social support system will expand exponentially as you meet new people through these experiences. If you are like Tré and Sharice and have a limited amount of time available, start with one of these activities, and try to select one that will maximize the likelihood that you will meet prospective friends. In other words, choose an activity that involves a high level of interaction with other people who share similar interests.

Find Couple Friends

Spend time with other couples that share similar values for commitment and togetherness. Of course, it is important to maintain friendships with single people as well. However, friendships with other couples provide valuable support for your marriage through both practical and emotional support. Going on double dates with other couples can provide you with new experiences and engaging conversations. In addition, you both can benefit from the emotional support you may receive from your friendships with other couples. Spending time with other couples will help you learn more about the dynamics of other couples' relationships and to gain ideas that you might apply to strengthen your own relationship. In the case of Tré and Sharice, they could meet another couple who lives in their neighborhood and invite that couple over to their home for a dinner party. Tré and Sharice would especially benefit by meeting another couple who recently relocated to the area, in that the two couples can then support each other through the similar transitions they face.

Maintain Individual Friendships after You Are Married

Encourage each other to nurture supportive friendships throughout the marriage. Individual friendships help partners maintain independent interests and values. Both of you probably have a number of friends who you knew long before you decided to get married, and these friendships can continue to be an important part of your life for years to come. Take advantage of the many means—such as e-mail, cell phones, instant messaging, visiting each other, or blogging—available to you to stay in touch with friends, especially if you live at a distance from them. Tré and Sharice may benefit from making extra efforts to reconnect with their individual friends in their previous hometown as a way to increase the support available to them in their marriage. It is healthy for you to have interests and experiences separate from your partner, because it keeps your relationship interesting.

Conclusion

Your marriage should connect you to the world and people around you—not isolate you. Build a support network to enhance your marriage through new experiences, opportunities, and connections with other people. Make efforts now and throughout your marriage to foster a social network to support you and the growth of your marriage.

Action Plan: Friendships and Social Support

1. Examine the current level of social support available to you in your relationship.

2. Seek out a supportive social network that includes people who provide a positive influence on you and your relationship.

3. Make efforts to reconnect with old friends with whom you may have lost touch over the years.

4. Enjoy new experiences and social groups as ways to expand your social network.

5. Maintain individual and couple friendships throughout your marriage.

Discussion Questions

1. How strong is your social network?

2. What is one thing you could do to improve your social network?

3. How important is it to you to have individual friends once you are married?

4. What are some problems that could arise for married couples that become isolated?

5. Who in your social network do you think is most supportive of your marriage?

Heather and Brad are getting married in three months. Brad is a banker and Heather is an attorney. Brad was recently offered a promotion in another city, which presented a great career opportunity for him. However, Heather has reservations about moving. She has worked hard to advance toward becoming a partner in her law firm, and she enjoys the firm in which she works.

The couple is deciding whether or not to move, and each partner is concerned about the career and family implications of their decision.

Heather is concerned that she will not find another firm that is as supportive of her work. She also enjoys their current community and living close to members of their extended families.

Brad's worry is that limited prospects exist for him to advance in his career in their current location, and he can't guarantee another opportunity will come along any time soon. He has felt ready to move on from his current job for the past year, but he has been unsuccessful in finding a better one in their hometown.

The couple knows that the decision they make will influence their careers and their marriage.

sixteen

Careers

Career issues have a direct and powerful impact on your marriage. Your career affects your marriage, and your marriage affects your career. Many premarital couples wish to discuss career-related issues—such as managing work stress and balancing two partners' careers—as they prepare to marry. A 2003 study published in the *Journal of Psychology and Theology* demonstrated that the most common problem newly married couples face is balancing work and family life. This chapter addresses these concerns and includes strategies to help you balance both your work and family life.

Careers and Marriage

Marriages often begin during busy times in partners' careers. Perhaps you are new to your career and just learning the ropes. Maybe you are in the midst of a major career transition or you may be established in your career and need to maintain your current level of productivity. Most people do not put their careers on hold to get married. Your job demands your time, energy, and attention—resources that are also needed to maintain a healthy marriage. Married couples experience many career-related issues that affect their relationships, including career decision-making, work/family spillover, challenges for dual-career couples, and career development. In this chapter, I describe each of these issues and then present some strategies couples can use to manage them.

Issue #1: Career Decision-Making

Once you are married, you must consider the impact of all career-related decisions on your spouse, as is evident in the case of Heather and Brad. Often, the best decision for one partner's career is not the best for the other's career. Career decisions also impact other aspects of a married couple's life. For example, if Brad were to take the new job in another city, both partners would have to give up the proximity they have to their extended families. Clearly, career decisions cannot be made without considering their impact on your entire life.

Career issues caused challenges for my husband and me early in our marriage. In fact, we struggled with career planning while on our honeymoon! At the time, we were deciding if we should leave our current graduate school program to pursue different career and educational plans elsewhere. We each applied for graduate programs in five cities, and we hoped to both be admitted to programs in the same city. Things did not work out as we hoped. Where I got in, my husband did not. Where my husband was accepted, I was not. Our two remaining choices were to remain in our current program or move to begin work elsewhere. We had many intense, challenging conversations during this time. Ultimately, we stayed put, but we learned of the difficulty of these decisions for newly married couples. In retrospect, this was the best decision we could have made, but it put a lot of strain on our marriage at the time.

You and your spouse will face many career-related decisions during your marriage. The following questions reflect the types of decisions you might face:

- Who will work?

- What type of work will each partner do?

- How will work arrangements change if and when you have children?

- What will happen if one spouse wishes to return to school?

- What will happen if one spouse decides to change career paths?

- Will spouses be able to do work at home, during free time?

- Would one partner be willing to relocate for the other partner to pursue a career opportunity?

- How would you handle differing levels of income?

When faced with these difficult decisions, many couples experience increased levels of stress and conflict in their relationships. Therefore, couples should develop strategies they can use to work together to resolve these challenging decisions. Two useful strategies for doing this include maintaining effective communication while discussing career issues and using negotiation and problem-solving skills.

Strategy: Maintain Effective Communication
Open communication is essential for maintaining a strong marriage in the face of career demands, so it's crucial to foster a respectful environment in which to address these concerns. You can do this by talking during times when both partners can give full attention to the conversation, listening carefully to what each partner has to say, thinking carefully before responding to one another, and agreeing upon a set of "ground rules" for managing disagreements. Review Chapters 2 and 4 for more information about effective communication and conflict management skills. My experience counseling couples and families has shown me over and over again that most people are much more likely to blame the other person during a conflict than

they are to examine their own role in the situation. Although at times it may be necessary to provide your partner with gentle reminders about keeping up the ground rules, your number one job while you are having difficult conversations with your partner is to monitor your own behavior. I suggest that you think carefully about the things you say, reflect often upon what you have said already, and take time during challenging career-related conversations to evaluate whether the conversation is headed into unhealthy territory.

Try your best to understand your partner's career expectations and needs, and be clear when you explain your expectations. Listen carefully when your partner raises concerns about the effects of your career on your marriage. It is difficult but extremely important to avoid becoming defensive when your partner raises concerns about your decisions and behaviors. Actor Alan Alda, famous for his role on the old television show *M*A*S*H*, and the author of the memoir *Never Have Your Dog Stuffed*, has provided some wonderful insights on listening. They can be summed up like this: You know that someone is really listening when they are listening with a willingness to change. Strive for that goal in your marriage.

When I counsel clients on how to begin difficult career-related conversations with someone they love, I suggest that they begin with an invitation for the other person to join the conversation when she is ready to do so. For example, if Brad wishes to start a conversation with Heather about moving to the new city for his job opportunity, he might say to her, "Heather, whenever it's a good time for you, I'd like to talk with you about our decision whether to move or not for my job." It's important to keep in mind that a good time to talk for you may not be a good time to talk for your partner. Both partners are more likely to be able to listen fully if the conversation happens at a time when there are minimal distractions and a clear understanding of mutual respect.

Heather and Brad would also benefit from setting aside some regular time to talk about the career-related decisions they are facing. Each partner should express his or her ideas clearly, and the listening partner can demonstrate respect by asking questions to help clarify the speaker's ideas and avoiding interrupting one another. When I work with couples and families who are facing challenging times in their relationships—like Heather and Brad's difficult career-related decisions—I often recommend that they schedule regular "check-ins" to see how the other one is doing. The details of these check-ins differ depending on the unique characteristics of each relationship. For example, one couple may find that it's helpful to set aside ten minutes after dinner every night. Another couple may decide to have a check-in conversation once a week, such as every Sunday evening as they relax for the week ahead. Even when it seems that these check-ins are no longer needed, it can be helpful to keep them up because they offer the time and permission that some couples need to talk about challenging topics.

Strategy: Use Negotiation and Problem-Solving Skills

Negotiation skills are essential when discussing career-related issues in marriage. Negotiating involves working together to develop a solution that takes into account each person's needs and desires, and good negotiations involve compromise and understanding between both partners. Each partner can begin by identifying his or her position, including the issues and needs that are most important to him or her. The ultimate outcome should be acceptable to both partners. It may be helpful for you to write down the possible solutions that are discussed as they come up to help you remember what you've already talked about and the strengths and weaknesses of each idea. In addition, writing down the final solution may help you and your partner ensure that you share a common understanding of what the solution means. In my counseling experiences, I frequently am amazed at how two people can have such vastly different views of the same incident or conversation! Although it may seem redundant to write down a solution that you've verbally agreed on, the additional clarity is likely to become very useful when it comes time to actually implement the decision you've made.

The problem-solving skills discussed in Chapter 10 will help you navigate the demands of work and family life. Career-related problems will arise in your marriage from time to time. Your effectiveness in managing these problems will determine how well you balance your careers with your family relationships. Review and practice the nine steps presented in Chapter 10 when you face career-related problems in your marriage.

Heather and Brad can apply negotiation and problem-solving skills to help them make a decision about whether or not to move for Brad's career opportunity. Heather and Brad can begin by giving themselves adequate time to think and discuss their options fully. For this couple in this situation, it's likely that they'll need several hours of conversations occurring over several weeks before they can reach a carefully thought-out decision. Because of the complexity of this situation for both partners—and especially Heather's career—the couple should resist the urge to make a hasty decision. Once they have set aside time to talk about the decision, they can begin to explore various possible solutions they can apply to this decision. For each solution, they should examine the likely outcomes and the degree to which the possible outcomes are acceptable to each partner. They may also keep a list of the solutions they discussed, and perhaps even create a "pros" and "cons" list to help them evaluate the potential outcomes for each possible solution. Heather and Brad would also benefit from prioritizing the importance of the various factors contributing to their decision, such as their proximity to family members, Heather's progress toward her goal of becoming a partner in her law firm, and Brad's career aspirations, including his desire to advance to a new position.

Work/Family Spillover

Work/family spillover occurs when tension or problems at work are carried home and taken out on family members. For example, you were angry because your boss belittled you during a meeting with colleagues, and when you came home, you made insensitive comments to your spouse. Because you spend a lot of time at your job, your work experiences have a big impact on your emotions. Sometimes, it is not possible to cheer up by the time you get home, so emotions that you experience on the job are often carried over into your family life. Everyone has a bad day at work from time to time, and it's normal to be affected by those experiences. However, if negative work-related emotions continue to spill over into a couple's marriage over time, it's likely to put a lot of stress onto that relationship.

Strategy: Set Boundaries

One strategy for managing work/family spillover is to establish boundaries between your career and your family life. This involves setting limits on the amount of time and energy you will devote to each area. Establishing boundaries involves creating a comfortable amount of space in your life for all of the things that are important to you. Leave work at work by keeping at least one evening each week work-free so you have time to spend with your spouse, and refrain from discussing work over dinner. Couples that work together face special challenges related to setting boundaries between their careers and family life. These couples need to develop clear career-related boundaries so their relationships do not become consumed by their shared work. The demands of every career are different. You and your partner may work together or in the same field, or you may have entirely dissimilar jobs in different fields. In any case, draw the lines that are most relevant to your relationship.

One additional note on boundaries: They are likely to change over time, and it's nearly impossible to maintain them perfectly. When a major deadline is looming, a person who usually avoids bringing work-related chores home may have to. However, this person should probably spend some extra time with his or her partner and friends once the deadline has passed. Work together with your partner to ensure a healthy balance between your career and relationship.

As an example of establishing positive boundaries between different areas of life, consider Heather's work as an attorney, and assume that she's been able to set a clear boundary between her work and her relationship with Brad. For example, she has set a personal rule for herself that she will turn off her BlackBerry when she walks out of the office. She also listens to relaxing music on her commute home so that she is "de-stressed" by the time she reaches the door before enjoying dinner with Brad. She has begun to take art classes on her own so that she feels that she has other things to talk about with Brad aside from her work. As a result of these steps, Heather is able to focus on her work while she is in her office, and she is able to avoid becoming stressed about work and enjoy herself while she is spending time with Brad. She is also able to talk with Brad about her interesting and challenging work-related experiences, but her work does not become an all-consuming topic of conversation.

Career Issue #3: Challenges for Dual-Career Couples

Dual-career couples are extremely common. The benefits that dual-career couples experience include opportunities for both partners to establish rewarding careers and a higher joint income. However, a dual-career lifestyle includes some unique demands. Balancing work and family needs is often overwhelming and challenging, especially for women, who may feel more pressure to focus primarily on their families and relationships over their career goals. Partners face other challenges—conflicts between work and family roles, the cost and scheduling of child care, implications of geographic moves, and competitiveness. Although each person enjoys an individual career path, the demands of two careers often place strain on marriages.

As my husband, Tom, and I have moved into our professional careers, the biggest challenge we face is finding time for our relationship. We are fortunate that both of us enjoy the work we do and receive a great deal of personal satisfaction from our jobs. However, our jobs keep us very busy. Between our hectic schedules filled with meetings, appointments, and the unique responsibilities of our jobs, there are some days in which we barely see each other between the time we wake up and go to sleep! We are constantly trying to figure out new ways to stay connected during the work week and make time for our relationship. Some of the things we've tried in the past include setting aside one night a week as a "date night," calling each other to check in during the day, taking walks together several mornings each week, and sharing a hug and kiss each day before we leave for work.

Strategy: Make Time for Your Partner Every Day

Create time for each other every day, no matter how little time that may be on certain days. Maintain close contact with your partner throughout the busy work week. Some couples call each other every day at lunchtime. Others always eat dinner together. Find a time that works in your relationship, and commit to spending it together. As an example, consider a couple that realizes that, between both partners' busy schedules, they are barely spending any time together. The man is a "night person," and his fiancée is a "morning person." The partners are both away from their home for most of the daytime hours, leaving very little time for them to connect. As a counselor, I would work with this couple to figure out a time that they can spend together in the midst of their busy lives. For example, the couple may decide to talk a walk together every evening at around 7 P.M. Over time, the couple will probably find that this time is very important in helping them stay connected despite their packed schedules. You may need to choose a time carefully, as the time that is best for you may not be best for your partner. For example, when my husband walks in the door after work, I'm ready to talk about my experiences that day, but he needs time to unwind before he's ready to talk. Over time, we arranged for him to have time to relax first, and then we spend time together later in the evening.

Even if you are only able to devote a few minutes to your partner on a particularly busy day, it's important to spend that time in a way that will help you feel connected to each other. Modern technology provides numerous options to help couples stay in communication with one another. Couples that can't be together physically over a period of time (whether that's one day or several weeks) should consider how they might use such methods as e-mail, instant messaging, cellular phones, and Web logs to stay connected during that time. Other, more "old-fashioned" strategies such as letter writing can also be helpful. These methods should not replace in-person contact, but they can help couples create a sense of connection when time is of the essence. I recently read in my local newspaper about an elderly couple who had been married for several decades who made homemade Valentine's Day cards for each other every year. They stated that these simple cards meant so much more to them than any store-bought card could mean. In your relationship, keep in mind that it's often the simple reminders and gestures that are most meaningful in helping you stay connected.

Career Issue #4: Career Development

Career development occurs over time, and plans often change as people progress in their careers. In the case of Heather and Brad, Heather is working toward becoming a partner in the law firm where she works, so she's trying to establish her reputation among her peers and potential clients. It is likely that Heather will face more significant implications of moving to another city now compared to later when she has already established a strong reputation and expertise in her particular area of law. Moving will have a unique set of consequences for Heather.

Developmental changes often present challenges for married couples. Sometimes, they require adjustments in the marriage—such as a change in the income level, a need to move to a different part of the country, a shift in the work schedule, and/or increased or decreased work responsibilities. Couples that do not maintain supportive relationships through these changes are likely to struggle. Just as career development influences family life, family development influences a person's career path, such as having a child or needing to take care of an elderly parent.

Strategy: Plan Ahead

Think about the career-related situations that may present challenges in your marriage over the coming years. Talk with people who are advanced in their careers in your profession to discover the difficulties they faced while balancing their families and careers. Although each person's career path is unique, it is likely that you will discover some common challenges that arise for people in your field of work. Complete the following exercise to examine how career developments may influence your marriage.

Directions: On a separate piece of paper, create a timeline including at least five significant events and goals that you would like to accomplish during your career. Write the tentative date by which you would like to accomplish each goal. Share your timelines with each other. How might the accomplishments on your timelines affect one another? Once you've discussed your timelines, keep them in a safe place so you can revisit them later and change them as your career plans change over time.

PARTNER A

Today's Date   Date of Retirement

_____   _____

_____

PARTNER B

Today's Date   Date of Retirement

_____   _____

_____

Think ahead toward the goals you have for your personal and professional lives. Consider the career and family transitions you and your spouse are likely to face together (e.g., moving, having children, or getting a promotion), and consider how you might handle them when they arise. Planning ahead helps minimize the struggles that career transitions present. You may find it helpful to plan a regular time each year during which you can take some time to review and update your career goals and plan for the future. Consider the typical ebb and flow of work in your profession, and identify some times during the year that you could devote to evaluating your career goals and development.

Heather and Brad may find that it is helpful for them to think about the decision they face now—whether to move for Brad's job opportunity—in light of the future goals they have for their careers and their family life. For example, Heather and Brad may be planning to have children soon after they are married, and one of them may be planning to become a full-time stay-at-home parent. In this case, the career goals of the partner who plans to continue to work may become a higher priority in order to maximize the family's financial stability once they become a single-income family. Any decision that Heather and Brad make about whether or not to move for Brad's job opportunity should take into account the goals and expectations that each partner has related to his or her future career plans.

Strategy: Use Available Support Systems

Many resources are available to help you manage the challenges you and your partner face in balancing career and family demands. It's quite common for people to wait to seek outside support until their problems have reached unmanageable proportions. I've worked with many clients who believed that the fact that they were seeking help from "an outsider" meant that something was wrong with them. However, as a counselor, I believe that people can benefit from outside support not only when they are experiencing major problems, but also when they want to figure out how to keep up with the things that are going well. There are some additional common warning signs that indicate it may be a good idea to seek support from outside of your relationship, whether that is from friends and family members or from professionals such as mental health professionals and career counselors. These warning signs include impasses in which it becomes impossible for a couple to resolve problems on their own, repeated attempts to make changes that seem to fail time after time, and situations in which the couple's resources and skills are inadequate for managing the problems they face.

You and your partner should identify friends, family members, and colleagues to whom you can turn for support in making career-related decisions. You can do this by reflecting on the people in your life who have been supportive of you in the past and considering how the support of those people is relevant to your current needs. Social support from family and friends can be invaluable when facing challenging decisions. Additional sources of support may be available through your employer or in your community. Many employers provide Employee Assistance Programs (EAP) to help employees manage stressors and challenges. If possible, work at a company known to have family-friendly policies. Community resources include career counselors, mental health professionals, and support groups.

Heather and Brad can seek out the support of their extended family members, as well as their friends, to help them make the difficult decision of whether or not to move. Although the couple will ultimately make the decision themselves, trusted confidantes can help the partners think through their choices and develop new possible solutions. Heather and Brad also may benefit from the services of a career counselor, a couples counselor, and/or a career mentor. Like Heather and Brad, you and your partner do not have to face career-related family problems alone. Seek out resources that could be helpful to you.

Conclusion

For many couples, balancing the demands of careers and family life is challenging. However, a rewarding career also presents many exciting and fulfilling opportunities to one or both partners. Set career-related boundaries in your marriage, and stick with them. Your career influences your marriage, and your marriage influences your career. The career-related decisions you face will present opportunities for your marriage to grow.

Action Plan: Careers

1. Consider the career-related decisions you are likely to face in the early years of your marriage.

2. Apply effective communication, conflict management, and problem-solving skills to help you manage career-related issues.

3. Create appropriate boundaries between your career and your marriage.

4. Plan ahead for long-term career issues that may develop.

5. Use support systems to assist you in managing career demands.

Discussion Questions

1. What are your most important career goals?

2. How can your partner support you in your career?

3. How easy or difficult do you anticipate it will be to balance work and marriage?

4. What do you think will be the most challenging aspects of balancing your career with marriage?

5. What strategies could you use to balance work and family life effectively?

Bill and Katherine have been married for ten years. They have two children in elementary school and both spouses work in professional jobs. Between taking the children to school and extracurricular activities, the demands of their jobs, and the responsibilities each has through community commitments, the couple's marriage seems to be just another responsibility.

Bill and Katherine often wonder where the fun has gone in their marriage. When they first married, they hoped to always laugh and share fun times together. At this point, they worry the fun has gone forever—or at least until retirement.

Everything in their marriage seems serious all the time—making arrangements for the children's activities, doing housework, and balancing everyone's schedules. Bill and Katherine still feel very much in love with each other but they wonder if their marriage will ever be fun again.

seventeen

Fun and Leisure

At this point in the book, marriage may seem complicated, overwhelming, and hard work. Many couples fear marriage will suck the fun from their relationships as in the case of Bill and Katherine. All too often, couples do let the fun slip away. Without fun, marriage becomes one more job to manage. Premarital couples may benefit from exploring the amount of fun and compatibility of leisure interests in their relationship. Strong relationships are based on enjoyment and happiness. As Judith Wallerstein and Sandra Blakeslee describe in their book *The Good Marriage*, "The nemesis of a good marriage is monotony unrelieved by imagination." In this chapter, we explore the fun aspects of marriage. I also present strategies couples can use when marriage loses the excitement and fun it once contained.

Marriage Is Fun!

Perhaps a more appropriate heading for this section would be "Marriage *Can Be* Fun!" Not all marriages are fun, and no marriage is fun all the time. Marriage takes work, but it involves fun times as well. Fun and laughter are common in satisfying marriages. There are many times when marriage is not enjoyable—such as during conflict. People who enter marriage with the expectation that marriage will be all fun will probably be disappointed. A more realistic goal is to aim for a relationship in which the good times outweigh the bad. A ratio of more positive interactions to negative interactions puts your marriage on course for success.

When I counsel couples, I often ask them to talk about the fun that exists in their relationship. After their initial shock related to having been asked this question (as in, "Isn't counseling supposed to be all about our problems?"), clients are usually able to share a number of positive experiences they've shared. Sometimes they have to think back a while, but I've worked with very few clients who have been unable to identify any fun experiences in their relationships. Usually, just thinking about shared fun experiences helps to create a more loving context in which couples can begin to create solutions for their current problems.

Fortunately, being married puts you at an advantage when it comes to having fun. You probably did not choose to marry your partner because he is boring to you. Most people select partners who are enjoyable and exciting to them. Most courtships are full of fun experiences that help the couple grow close. Think back to all the dates and experiences you've shared with your partner so far. Most of them were probably enjoyable; otherwise, you would not have been likely to continue your relationship. Partners also often share interests with one another. Even partners who have different interests can share fun times together, as each partner introduces the other to new experiences. A spouse is a great buddy for sharing new and exciting adventures.

Marriage provides many opportunities for good times due to the amount of time you spend together. Your partner is often around to share the funny moments in your day-to-day life—such as being goofy at home, reliving amusing situations that happened at work, and noticing the ironies in the world around you. When you are married, you are also likely to experience more causes for celebration—anniversaries, promotions, financial successes, and more—simply because there are now two individual's accomplishments to celebrate. All of these fun experiences keep the excitement alive.

How Does Marriage Lose Its Fun?

Sometimes life takes over and marriage becomes less fun and less exciting. As Bill and Katherine in the case study at the beginning of the chapter found, keeping up the fun in marriage becomes evermore challenging when also balancing the demands of work, parenting, and community involvement. Couples can lose the enjoyment in their marriage for many reasons. First, partners often take one another for granted. People often become consumed by other parts of their lives, assuming that their marriages will remain strong. However, neglecting your partner leads you to forget the enjoyable and attractive characteristics you appreciated in the beginning of your relationship.

Second, married couples often sink into routines that create monotony in their relationships. Every day begins to feel the same as the last—get up, get dressed, go to work, come home, eat dinner, watch television, then go to bed. This form of monotony seeps into marriage and eliminates the fun and newness of the relationship. Bill and Katherine have probably developed a daily schedule that allows them to manage all of the demands on their time—and yet the schedule also limits the flexibility and spontaneity in their daily experiences.

Third, partners sometimes stop changing and growing individually. New experiences fade and partners lack personal growth. Your partner becomes predictable. For example, I often can predict what my husband will say before he says it—and vice versa. While some predictability is nice, too much is boring. I am happy to report that my husband still manages to surprise me on a regular basis, and I enjoy learning new things about him every day. However, when partners experience a stagnant period in their growth, the impact on the relationship can be boredom and missed opportunities for fun.

Finally, marriage becomes less fun when consumed by negativity and conflict. You cannot easily laugh with your partner when you feel angry with him or her—and attempts at humor during conflict often make matters worse. In some marriages, negativity becomes a way of life. Negative interactions become a vicious cycle that is difficult to break. Partners grow resentful and angry toward one another, yet they lack the skills to change these damaging patterns. Once a couple gets caught in this vicious and damaging cycle of negativity, it becomes nearly impossible for them to enjoy each other's company. If you ever recognize this pattern happening in your relationship, I encourage you to seek couples counseling to help you develop a more positive context for your marriage.

How Can Marriage Become More Fun?

Make efforts to create a fun marriage and enjoy your partner. You and your partner can enjoy many entertaining and leisurely activities together—such as dancing, dining out, going to parties with friends, playing board games, going to a nature park, exercising together, going to plays and concerts, visiting local attractions like a zoo or museum, or shopping—just to name a few. In this section, I present steps to increase the fun in your relationship.

Create Time to Devote to Fun

Set aside time to share fun and leisure with your partner. This is especially important if your relationship becomes monotonous and routine. Carve out time for fun to keep your marriage fresh and exciting. Your connection to one another grows stronger as you share positive, enjoyable experiences together. Katherine and Bill might decide to spend just ten to fifteen minutes a day doing something fun together—playing a game, watching a funny television show, or laughing with their children. Once they become more accustomed to spending this time together, they can begin to add more time for fun as their schedules permit.

Enjoy the Simple Moments of Pleasure in Marriage

Take pleasure in the small, joyful moments in your relationship. Fun does not need to come with a hefty price tag. It can come from lounging in bed with your partner on a weekend morning, from renting a funny movie and watching it together, or from making up silly songs to sing together. I hope that you and your partner feel comfortable enough to act goofy in front of each other without having to worry about being judged. Pay attention to the enjoyable moments you already share—even if they are as simple as going out to eat or hanging out with friends. Often, fun moments exist right before your eyes, but you are too busy or preoccupied to see them. I encourage you to spend relaxing time with your partner so you'll be more able to notice these pleasurable moments as they arise.

Celebrate Your Growth and Progress

Celebrate the major and minor accomplishments you share as a couple. It is great to celebrate special days like anniversaries or birthdays. However, your celebrations need not be limited to monumental events, and you can create your own fun and unique ways of celebrating special occasions with your partner. Celebrate once all your wedding plans are in order. Celebrate when you go a week without a fight during a challenging time in your marriage. Celebrate when you communicate effectively about a difficult subject. A healthy relationship is always cause for celebration.

Use Humor—with Caution

Humor is a great stress reducer, which helps couples release tension. Laughter actually creates physiological reactions that reduce stress and enhance relaxation. Sharing laughter with your partner helps you relax and enjoy each other. I have heard most of my husband's jokes many, many times by now (I can usually say the punch line along with him!), but they still usually manage to bring a smile to my face. Be cautious when using humor, however, because it can be offensive or hurtful. Be especially careful when using humor during a conflict, because it may come across as insensitive, veiled criticism. Making fun of your partner is never funny (it is actually a type of emotional abuse), and it almost always causes more damage than good. Seek outside sources of humor—such as watching a funny television show together, people watching at the mall, playing with a puppy, or playing a new game that neither one of you is good at—as opposed to making jokes about your partner or your relationship. Use humor to diffuse tension, rather than to create anger or hostility.

Be Creative and Adventurous

Try new things with your partner and create more opportunities for fun. Brainstorm a list of new ways to have fun together. Don't get stuck in a rut of always doing the same thing for fun (e.g., going to dinner and a movie). As much as you enjoy your favorite activity, you can expand your opportunities for having fun by seeking out new adventures and experiences. Katherine and Bill could benefit from trying a new activity with their children, such as bowling or dancing. The fun in your relationship can also occur with other people!

Share Fun Memories from the Past

In order to create fun in the present, sometimes it is helpful to turn to the past to remember good times in your relationship. Recall the early days of your relationship and the experiences you used to enjoy together. These past experiences provide clues for ways to increase the fun in your relationship now, and they also offer hope for a more fun future. So, take some time to reminisce about amusing experiences you've had in the past or to peruse old photo albums to help you remember the good times you have shared.

Have Separate and Shared Interests

It is healthy for married partners to maintain shared and individual leisure interests. Nurture your individual growth within your marriage by taking part in activities that you enjoy alone. During vacations with your partner, it can be especially important to spend some time alone. Spending all your time with your partner may create tension, especially if you and your partner have different interests. By spending time nurturing your own interests—at home or on vacation—you enhance your relationship as you grow with each new experience. Complete the following exercise to examine the shared and individual leisure interests within your relationship.

Directions: The following diagram represents separate and shared leisure activities and interests. In the middle space, write down the activities that you enjoy doing together for fun. In the spaces on the side, write down the separate activities that you enjoy doing on your own. If you notice an imbalance in the number of activities in the different sections, discover new interests to enjoy together or separately.

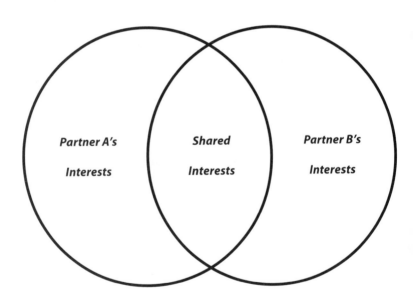

Partner A's   *Shared*   *Partner B's*

Interests   *Interests*   *Interests*

Conclusion

Make marriage enjoyable for both of you. Although marriage involves work, don't let the fun slip away from your relationship once you get married. Marriage becomes miserable when it is all work and no play. Leisure activities that provide you with new experiences, personal growth, laughter, and enjoyment are likely to have a positive impact on your mental health *and* your relationship. Although you cannot expect to have fun all the time, maintain a healthy amount of enjoyment in your relationship. Build on this enjoyment once you are married. For all the talk about how much work marriage involves, it can also provide good times. A marriage with no fun is not a happy marriage!

Action Plan: Fun and Leisure

1. Recognize that marriage can be enjoyable, although it also involves work and challenging times.

2. Create more fun in your marriage by devoting time to pleasurable, simple moments together, celebrating often, using humor appropriately, sharing creativity and adventure, reminiscing about past enjoyable experiences , and maintaining individual and shared interests.

Discussion Questions

1. What is the most fun experience you have shared with your partner?

2. How does your partner add fun to your life?

3. What would you do if your marriage lost its excitement?

4. What fun and leisure activities do you or could you enjoy together?

5. How will maintaining separate interests help your relationship?

When Shawn proposed, Mary Jane thought saying "yes" was the right thing to do, but now she is not so sure.

Mary Jane and Shawn have always had a volatile relationship—intense fights and intense passion and love. Lately, the fights have gotten worse, and the couple cannot seem to agree on anything. It seems to Mary Jane that she fights with Shawn about everything—the wedding plans, their families and friends, how they spend time together on the weekends, their finances, and the list goes on.

Mary Jane wonders if she should end the engagement, but she's not sure what she wants for their relationship. Although she feels pretty certain that they are not ready for marriage, Mary Jane doesn't know how to talk with Shawn about these concerns. He continues to seem focused on going through with the wedding, and she is worried about hurting his feelings by raising these concerns with him.

eighteen
Disengagement

Some couples make the difficult decision to call off their engagements, particularly after careful consideration of their compatibility in the issues discussed in this book. Although this is a painful decision, it is the best decision for some couples. One difficult aspect of calling off an engagement is that the couple has already put effort into planning the wedding. The couple, or their family members, may have already invested a good deal of money into the wedding, and much of that investment may not be refundable if the wedding is canceled. In addition, many people are afraid of the embarrassment they may face in telling other people in their lives that the wedding has been canceled, especially if wedding invitations have already been mailed and a wedding shower has already been thrown.

Calling off an engagement is more complex than ending a dating relationship. There is a high level of commitment between engaged partners, and the couple has probably established dreams and plans for their future. The couple may have already completed wedding arrangements—such as reserving venues for the ceremony and reception, purchasing a wedding gown, and paying nonrefundable down payments for the caterers, flowers, and disc jockey. If invitations were mailed already to hundreds of invitees, the pressure to go through with the wedding is especially intense.

The end of an engagement does not necessarily signify the end of the relationship. Some couples do decide not to continue their relationships. However, other couples decide to postpone their wedding plans, return to dating, and then revisit the idea of engagement at a later time. Other previously engaged couples stay together indefinitely and never marry. Any of these outcomes are challenging for a couple, especially if partners do not agree about the expectations for the relationship. In this chapter, I discuss possible reasons for canceling an engagement and suggestions for surviving the end of an engagement.

When to Call It Off

Calling off an engagement can be a wise, mature decision. Ending an engagement is much less costly—both emotionally and financially—than going through a divorce. The reasons for ending a premarital relationship vary and may include poor communication, decreased love between the partners, and the realization that partners hold different attitudes toward marriage. Most often, more than one reason leads to the termination of a premarital relationship, and partners in the same relationship often view the reasons for the breakup differently. Some valid reasons for postponing or ending an engagement include deep problems existing in the relationship, partners recognizing that they are not ready for marriage, the presence of practical barriers, and the partners discovering major irreconcilable differences.

You are the only person who can make the decision as to whether it is right for you to cancel your engagement and wedding. As a counselor, when I work with individuals who are considering ending a relationship, I can't make that decision for them. However, I have talked through these decisions with a number of clients, and some end up staying in their relationships, while others decide that it would be best to leave their partners. Although you will probably hear the opinions of many friends and family members as to whether or not you should stay in your relationship, the ultimate decision will be your own. Make sure that you spend enough time considering all of the alternative outcomes before you make this potentially life-changing decision.

Deep problems that exist within a relationship do not go away just because a couple marries. Major problems include physical, verbal, or emotional abuse, substance abuse, infidelity, and/or major patterns of negative conflict within the relationship. Each of these problems requires serious attention and treatment, and each is a warning sign of a relationship that is not ready for marriage. If one or more of these problems exist within your relationship, seek help immediately. Recognize that these unhealthy patterns are likely to worsen over time unless both partners commit to change and treatment.

Sometimes, one or both partners recognize that they are not ready for such a serious commitment as marriage. This situation is especially difficult if one partner is ready, while the other partner is not. Both partners need to be committed fully to making the marriage work. It is normal to feel less that 100 percent ready to marry. Some doubts are natural, and marriage is indeed a somewhat scary unknown. However, pervasive thoughts of doubt and fear indicate a need to re-evaluate whether marriage is the right step for the relationship right now.

Often, practical reasons necessitate the end of an engagement. Although some couples have healthy relationships and feel ready to commit to marriage, practical matters must often be settled before marriage becomes a wise step. For example, an individual might wish to become established in a career before marrying, especially if the career involves long hours and travel. Another person may wish to save enough money before getting married so that the couple enters marriage with financial security. Individuals often feel a need to be settled in their own lives before they join their lives with someone else.

Finally, some couples discover during their engagements that they differ irreconcilably in their views on important subjects.

For example, one partner wants children, and the other does not. Perhaps a person discovers that her fiancé expects her to sacrifice major career goals for the marriage, and that person is unwilling to make that sacrifice. Or a couple cannot reconcile differing religious beliefs. When couples cannot agree on these core issues, they may decide not to pursue marriage. Unfortunately, compromise is not always possible in a relationship.

Some people may wonder how and why couples in any of these situations would agree to get engaged in the first place. It may seem that these differences should have been obvious from the beginning of the couple's courtship. However, this is not always that case. First, remember that couples often are swept away by the romance of a new relationship. Most people focus on the positive aspects of a new relationship—the excitement and fantasy that surround a new love. Second, some of these problems do not appear relevant until they are considered in light of marriage. For example, religious differences might not seem important during the early stages of a relationship. Once the notion of marriage enters the picture, relationship problems take on a whole new meaning. For these reasons, then, calling off an engagement is not an indication that a person is weak, unintelligent, or immature. Again, this decision is often a sign of strength, wisdom, and careful deliberation.

Calling Off an Engagement

If you make the decision that you wish to end your relationship with your fiancé, plan carefully how to share your decision with your partner. If you do not feel safe sharing this decision alone in a private place, arrange to meet your partner in a public location (such as a restaurant or coffee shop) or to share the decision in the presence of a trusted friend or counselor. Assume that your partner will be unhappy to hear this news—although there is a possibility that your partner may feel relief if she was having similar doubts. Emphasize your reasons for coming to this decision, and if possible, explain the efforts you made as you went through the decision-making process. However, be clear that the decision was yours, even if you discussed your decision with other people. In addition, let your partner know what you plan to do in order to manage any practical arrangements that need to be made (for example, canceling wedding vendors, notifying friends and family members, or putting a stop to any legal proceedings that may have begun). Finally, be respectful of your partner's potential needs for time and space in order to determine how to proceed with your relationship.

If you are on the other end of this decision—your partner tells you that she wants to call off your engagement—do your best to remain calm during this conversation so that you are able to think clearly about your needs. If you do not feel that you are in the right state of mind to carry on a long conversation, let your partner know how much time and space you might need in order to process her decision. As much as possible, think through the practical details that have gone into planning the wedding thus far, and identify your needs in the situation. Be clear in making any requests to your partner regarding tasks you would like her to complete or financial issues. Take the time you need to make decisions about how you would like your relationship to proceed following your partner's disclosure of her decision.

When it is time to announce the end of the engagement to friends and family, do so carefully and on your own time schedule. I recommend that you begin by sharing the news with a small number of people who you are confident will be supportive of you and will listen empathically to your story. Then, enlist the support of those people to help you determine the best strategy for sharing the news more broadly. You may want to send a written note to people who have been invited to the wedding to explain that the wedding has been cancelled and you would appreciate their support during this difficult time. If you would like for the people in your life to respect your privacy, make that clear as well. You are not obligated to share any details you do not want to share with anyone. Other practical considerations you may face during this time involve returning wedding gifts you have received already, taking time off from your job in order to regroup, and dealing with gossip that may arise related to your relationship. Through all of these challenges, rely on the support of people who provide a positive influence for you, and avoid those people who wish to judge you, your former partner, or your decision.

Surviving the End of an Engagement

In any context, the end of a relationship is a stressful, painful process. Breakups are more stressful when there was a high level of commitment to the relationship, so the end of an engagement is likely to cause both partners a great deal of turmoil. According to the book *Premarital Prediction of Marital Quality or Breakup*, by Thomas B. Holman, women are more likely than men to end premarital relationships. However, a relationship ended by a partner of either gender involves a difficult process of seeking closure for the past and moving forward to new relationships. If one partner does not want the relationship to end, that person will probably experience more stress, regardless of gender. However, a breakup is also likely to be difficult for the person who wanted to end the relationship. In this section, I discuss several strategies to help you get through this difficult transition, particularly if the end of the engagement also signifies the end of the relationship.

Take the Time You Need
No hard and fast rules dictate how long it should take you to move on following a breakup or the end of an engagement.

Move forward slowly and at your own pace. Many factors interact to determine the amount of time it will take before you feel at peace with the breakup—such as the degree to which you wanted the breakup, the length of your relationship, the strength of your support system, and the amount of activity in other aspects of your life. Don't rush to "get over it" or "move on," even if you feel pressure to do so from friends or family members. Expect to feel upset about the breakup for a while. Appreciate the small steps you take in moving forward with your life. Ultimately, those small steps will become bigger and bigger movements toward your new future.

Nurture Your Other Relationships

Seek out a support system to help you through this difficult transition. While you were engaged and dating, you may not have had much spare time to devote to your family and friends. With the end of your engagement, you now have time to spend with other important people in your life. These relationships are essential to helping you maintain connections during a time when you may feel disconnected. Take this opportunity to enjoy the many other relationships in your life. Be cautious, however, about spending significant amounts of time with friends or family members who appear to be impatient with you or are demeaning to you or your partner. You may feel some sense of enjoyment in participating in a verbal bashing of your former partner with other people. However, this negativity can actually make it more difficult to move on, in that you probably still have some positive memories and emotions related to your partner.

Learn the Lessons from Your Relationship and Breakup

Seize this valuable opportunity to learn about yourself through this transition. Ask yourself, "What can I learn from this experience?" and, "What can I do differently now that I know what I learned from this relationship?" You can learn many lessons by examining the role you played in your relationship and its breakup. Maybe you can recognize warning signs to look out for in future relationships. Perhaps you will discover some changes you could make to become a better person. You may also discover that the relationship has changed you—for better or for worse. Any lessons you learn will help you move forward and continue to grow.

Seek Counseling

A counselor can help you examine your past relationships and explore future opportunities. Ending an engagement is a huge transition. With it, you move away from a set of plans for your future, and it may be challenging to sort through your thoughts and feelings. A counselor can assist you in making sense of the past and in moving forward. Working with a counselor during a time of relationship transition can be particularly helpful because a counselor can be a more objective source of support than most of the people in your life who are already very familiar with your situation. Seek a trusted counselor to help you process the major transition you face.

Build New Dreams for Your Future

Eventually, you will be ready to move forward with your life—with or without your former partner. When you reach this point, you have an exciting opportunity to create plans for a new life and a bright future. Your dreams may be very different from the dreams you shared with your partner, and you now have the chance to create your life on your own terms. You are likely to have grown from the challenges you faced through your relationship transition, and you can apply these lessons to help you experience your life in a new way. Take advantage of new opportunities, and follow your dreams for a fulfilling phase in your life.

Conclusion

If your engagement ends, you will survive! Many people will say to you, "Be glad this happened now, and not after you were married." You may hate to hear this again, but there is undeniable truth to that statement. Ending a marriage is much more costly and complicated than ending an engagement—even when you must call off an elaborate wedding. Most likely, if your relationship could not survive engagement, it would not have survived marriage. Although it is a painful experience, ending an engagement is wise if the relationship is not ready for such a major step. If you are in this situation, care for yourself, and move forward at your own pace. Trust that the future holds even brighter possibilities for you.

Action Plan: Disengagement

1. Understand that ending an engagement can be a wise decision for couples in which there are individual, relationship, or practical issues that would impact the couples' ability to create a positive, lasting marriage.

2. The end of an engagement does not necessarily signify the end of the relationship, but it does indicate a new phase in your life regardless of whether the relationship continues or not.

3. If your engagement ends, work through that experience by being patient with yourself, strengthening positive relationships with others, learning from your experiences, seeking counseling, and building new dreams for your life.

Ethan and Marie are preparing for their wedding, which is now five months away. They are required to attend two premarital counseling sessions with the minister who will marry them at their church. They were told by their minister that most of these sessions will involve talking about plans for the wedding ceremony.

However, Ethan and Marie would like to spend more time in premarital counseling talking about their relationship and preparing for their upcoming marriage. They are unsure whether their minister could provide them with this more in-depth approach to premarital counseling, but they also do not know about any other resources available to find the type of counseling that they believe would be most beneficial for their relationship.

nineteen

A Consumer's Guide to Premarital Counseling

Throughout the time that I have researched premarital counseling, many people have described to me their personal experiences as clients in premarital counseling. Their stories range from the life-enriching to the horrifying. From these stories, I know there are some very good premarital counselors out there who love to help couples prepare for marriage and take great pride in their work. However, some providers of premarital counseling are much less effective, and some could potentially be causing harm to the couples they counsel. For that reason, this chapter presents important considerations to help you select a premarital counseling provider. Also, I describe some available premarital counseling programs and other helpful resources.

Premarital counseling programs aim to develop your strengths as a couple, not to dredge up new or old problems in your relationship. Couples that attend premarital counseling may experience the following benefits: increased thoughtfulness about marriage, identification of resources for later assistance, and the prevention of later distress. Many couples that participate in premarital counseling view it as a helpful experience. Your needs for a premarital counseling program will depend on your background as an individual and as a couple. The number of options available to you for premarital counseling can be overwhelming for couples that are already balancing planning their weddings with many other areas of their lives. Therefore, I offer the information provided in this chapter to help you sort through the available options to determine the provider and program format that will be most beneficial to you and your partner. This chapter helps you to find the best program to help you prepare for marriage.

Some couples face requirements for the type of premarital preparation they must receive. For example, many couples that marry in a religious institution must attend premarital counseling sessions with a clergyperson. Other couples live in a state in which the government implemented restrictions on the providers and formats of premarital counseling programs. For example, at the time of this writing the Florida state government passed legislation that allows couples that participated in a premarital preparation program to receive a discount on their marriage licenses. The program they attend must meet for at least four hours and cover the following four topics: communication skills, conflict resolution, parenting and children, and finances. If you face such restrictions, you can always go above and beyond any minimal requirements. For example, if you must attend a group counseling program through your religious institution, you might also request individual counseling sessions with your clergyperson. If that is not possible, you may receive individual premarital counseling from a mental health professional in your community. Select a premarital counseling provider and program that are most suitable for meeting the needs of your upcoming marriage.

Deciding on a Premarital Counseling Provider

Many types of professionals provide premarital counseling. Although most couples receive premarital counseling from a clergyperson, other options exist if you are not affiliated with a religious institution or if you prefer to receive your premarital counseling elsewhere. Other professionals who may be qualified to provide premarital counseling include marriage and family counselors and therapists, mental health counselors, family life educators, social workers, and psychologists. Also, some religious institutions train other leaders to provide premarital counseling. Finally, some providers of premarital counseling are married couples that serve as mentors to engaged couples.

Membership in one of the groups listed previously does not automatically signify that a person received training or experience in providing premarital counseling. In fact, many people who provide premarital counseling have never been trained in it. In my survey of more than 200 premarital counseling providers, nearly one-third of the providers never received any form of specialized professional training in premarital counseling. What they lack in training, many make up for in experience. The providers in my survey averaged almost twenty years' experience providing premarital counseling. Many premarital counseling providers have helped numerous couples over the years prepare for marriage, and they have experience helping couples consider the same issues you face in your relationship.

To help you decide on a premarital counseling provider, ask the following questions of the providers you are considering.

What Training and Experience Related to Premarital Counseling Do You Have?

Providers vary in their degree of experience related to premarital counseling. How would you decide, for example, between the following premarital counseling providers: a licensed marriage and family therapist who has years of experience counseling married couples, but never before provided *premarital* counseling, a clergyperson who has thirty years of experience providing premarital counseling but never received formal professional training in premarital counseling, or a third provider who is conducting his or her first premarital counseling program after recently receiving a certification in a widely used premarital counseling program.

Which provider offers the best service? It's not possible to tell from the information provided here. Unfortunately, no widely accepted standards exist related to the qualifications necessary to provide premarital counseling. Ask any provider with whom you might work to describe his or her experience. If you are in a special situation—such as entering a second marriage or getting married after you already have children—ask if the provider has experience working with couples like you.

Another consideration is whether the provider has a personality that clicks with you and your partner. You and your partner may prefer someone who is less talkative and allows you to do most of the talking. You may prefer a male, a female, or a team with one male and one female. You and your partner should both be comfortable with your selected provider. For example, a former student of mine once shared with me that her premarital counseling provider spent most of their counseling sessions talking about fishing with her then-fiancé (who later became her ex-husband). Although her fiancé probably felt comfortable with that provider at that time, she clearly didn't feel comfortable with that person—not even comfortable enough to share her dissatisfaction with the services they received.

What Is Your Approach to Premarital Counseling?

As I discuss later in this chapter, there are several approaches to premarital counseling. Some providers prefer an educational premarital counseling program in which they teach you lessons about relationship skills. These providers may like to work from a formal curriculum. Others prefer an informal, unstructured approach that addresses each need as it arises within the sessions. Other providers use a different approach with every couple, depending on the needs and preferences of the couple.

Some premarital counseling providers practice from a particular theoretical framework. For example, some providers offer cognitive-behavioral counseling, in which they help you increase the thinking patterns and behaviors that are conducive to a satisfying marriage. Other providers practice from a family systems theory perspective. In this type of counseling, the focus is on identifying patterns within your families-of-origin that influence your current relationship. Still other providers use a solution-focused theoretical framework for practicing premarital counseling. Through this perspective, the provider helps you identify resources for solving future problems that arise in your relationship. Many other approaches to premarital counseling exist, and you should find a provider who offers an approach that suits your and your partner's outlooks on life. Also, your premarital counseling provider should be able to explain his or her theoretical approach to you in language that you can understand. A provider's failure to respond openly and clearly to your questions about her qualifications is a red flag that her services should be avoided.

How Many Sessions Will There Be? What Is the Cost?

Agree on these practical issues before you begin to work with a provider. The premarital counseling providers in my survey spend anywhere from one to eighty hours with each couple in premarital counseling, and the average length was about eight hours. One hour may not be nearly enough time for you, and eighty hours might be impossible to schedule into your busy lives. Your provider may have a time frame in which he likes to work with couples. However, your needs and schedule may necessitate a shorter or longer program. Agree on a length of time at the beginning so you and your provider know how much time is available to spend on each issue. For example, if you only have five hours available with your premarital counselor, you would not want to spend four hours discussing one topic if you have other important issues to address. Your provider may agree to alter the time frame later, but having a general idea about the time you will spend in counseling will help you pace your sessions from the outset.

Also, discuss the cost of the program with your provider. Costs vary depending on the format, setting, and provider. Many clergypersons provide free premarital counseling to their parishioners, although some charge a small fee or donation, particularly if you are not a member of their religious institution. In some communities, free or low-cost programs are available through government or community agencies. If you choose to attend premarital counseling with a mental health professional in your community, you might pay his or her usual fee for a counseling session. However, some mental health professionals offer free or low-cost premarital counseling as a service to the community. Group programs are usually less expensive than individual programs, as the group program allows you to share the cost. Because costs vary, discuss the cost with your provider up front so you can make an informed decision about how much you are able to afford. If your hearts are set on a particular program and provider but you are unable to afford it, ask a friend or family member if they would be willing to pay for your premarital counseling as your wedding gift. I can't think of a better gift than time shared with your partner working to create a happy, successful marriage!

Which Topics Will We Discuss?

Based on your provider's approach to premarital counseling, she will believe that certain topics are most important to discuss with you. Your provider might be an expert or have received extensive training in some issues. For example, a clergyperson might have strong skills in helping couples develop a spiritual foundation for their marriage. A provider with expertise in certain topics may be less knowledgeable in other areas. For example, while a marriage and family therapist may help you to communicate effectively about money, it is unlikely that she will offer specific advice about allocating your retirement funds. For this topic, you would need to seek the services of a financial planner.

If you have special needs, find out how flexible your provider is willing to be in discussing the topics that are most important to you. Tell your premarital counseling provider which topics you want to discuss either during or before your first session. You might also establish objectives related to each of the topics you want to discuss. For example, you may want to discuss parenting. Your specific objective is to agree on individual goals you each want to attain before you become parents. If you are clear with your provider, you increase the likelihood that he will meet your needs.

What Do You Think Are the Most Important Things to Do to Prepare for Marriage?

Your provider's answer to this question gives you an idea about his or her values related to marriage. Marriage is a topic laden with values and expectations, especially for professionals who work with families. Find a premarital counselor whose marriage and family-related values are similar to your own. At the very least, your premarital counselor should respect your and your partner's values for marriage, and particularly your vision for your future marriage. Look for a provider who believes all marriages are unique and special, and that provider will help you appreciate the unique and special aspects of your marriage.

Deciding on a Premarital Counseling Program

There are two ways to classify premarital counseling programs: the degree to which the format is structured, and the number of participants in the program. The structure and format of premarital counseling programs can be standardized or individualized. Standardized programs are based on a protocol, which provides a set curriculum for all couples that enter the program. Many standardized programs are supported by scientific research, and they tend to address the most common issues and skills that engaged couples are interested in learning. These programs are often structured, have a set format for the topics and skills they address, and occur within a previously established time period.

Individualized programs, on the other hand, tend to be less structured. A premarital counseling provider who offers an individualized program may have no set agenda for the topics and/or format of the counseling sessions. Rather, the provider uses an open-ended discussion format to raise the most important issues for each couple. Providers of individualized programs may guide couples through some structured exercises to address the specific needs of each couple.

Programs can be conducted with either a group or an individual couple, and some programs combine some group meetings with additional individual meetings. In a group program, several engaged couples meet at once, and a facilitator or team of facilitators guides the group through discussions, educational information, and skill-building exercises. A benefit of a group format is that couples share their experiences and learn from one another. Programs can also be conducted with an individual couple. Advantages of individual programs are that they allow you to go in-depth into the issues related to your marriage, and they allow you to have the undivided attention of your premarital counseling provider. The following list represents four categories of premarital counseling.

Types of Premarital Counseling Programs

- Standardized program with a group

- Individualized program with a group

- Standardized program with an individual couple

- Individualized program with an individual couple

Some research has compared the effectiveness of standardized programs with individualized programs. A study published in *Family Relations* in 2001 showed that couples that attended a standardized program were more likely to benefit from the program. However, it is difficult to research individualized programs because they are so unique, which means they are less compatible with standardized measurements used in premarital counseling outcome research. Other researchers argue that standardized programs are not the most useful format for addressing each engaged couple's specific needs. Therefore, it is not possible at this time to determine which type of program is more effective for all couples. Both types of programs can be effective depending on the needs of each couple, and your preferences will determine the program that is right for you. Consider which type of program appeals to you and is most appropriate for your current needs. The following exercise helps you consider the type of program that will be most useful to you.

Directions: Select the response that is most true for you. Ask your partner to do the same. Scoring directions are at the end of the exercise.

▶ 1. **I would prefer that my time in premarital counseling:**

   A.   Is spent with my partner alone

   B.   Is spent sharing ideas and experiences with other engaged couples

▶ 2. **The most important thing I would like to gain from a premarital counseling program is:**

   A.   A deeper understanding of my relationship

   B.   A set of new skills that I can use in my relationship

▶ 3. **My fiancé and I:**

   A.   Have some specific conflict areas that we need to resolve before we marry

   B.   Do not have any major conflicts that we need to resolve before we marry

▶ 4. **My partner and I are so busy that we rarely get to spend time alone**

   A.   Mostly true

   B.   Mostly false

▶ 5. **I would feel uncomfortable discussing some of the premarital counseling topics in this book in front of a group.**

   A.   True

   B.   False

▶ 6. **When I am communicating about difficult issues with my partner, I prefer:**

   A.   A lot of flexibility and free-flowing conversation

   B.   A lot of structure to guide the conversation

CONTINUE

▶ **7.** **I believe that my needs for premarital counseling are:**

    A.   Probably different from the needs of other couples

    B.   Relatively similar to the needs of other couples

▶ **8.** **I think that the best way to learn how to improve my relationship is by:**

    A.   Discussing with my partner what we would like to change

    B.   Learning what has worked for other couples in improving their relationships

Scoring Directions: You will have two separate scores for this quiz. First, add up all of your A and B answers for questions 2, 3, 6, and 7. If you have more A answers, then you prefer an individualized program with less structure. If you have more B answers, then you prefer a standardized program that is more structured.

Next, add up all your A and B answers for questions 1, 4, 5, and 8. If you have more answers marked A, then you prefer a program in which you and your partner work individually with a premarital counselor. If you have more B answers, then you prefer a program where you meet with a group of other couples.

If you have an even number of A and B answers for either section, then either type of program might work for you.

Now, compare your and your partner's scores. If you have similar scores, you have a good idea about the type of program that is right for your relationship. If, however, your scores are different, go back through the questions and discuss which program characteristics are most important to each of you. You could benefit from attending a combination of two different types of programs. For example, attend a group program and meet with the program leader individually. Another alternative is to show your responses to this exercise to your premarital counseling provider, and discuss how she might adapt the program to meet both of your needs.

Seize every opportunity to work on your relationship while you are engaged. Opportunities abound for couples to explore their relationships during this time period. Many high-quality standardized programs exist, and there are also many options for individualized counseling. By completing the previous exercise, you will have an idea of the type of program that will be most helpful to you. To help you evaluate the options available to you for premarital counseling, consider the following questions.

What Are the Qualifications of the Leader of the Program?

Even if you participate in a program that is well established in your community, ask your provider the same questions listed previously. Get a feel for the provider's style, and see if it is a good match with your needs. Also, make sure that he has received adequate training and experience in conducting the specific program you will attend. A provider who is new to a particular program or approach often works under the guidance of a supervisor. Although the supervisor may not be present at the sessions, the availability of a supervisor is a good sign that the provider will deliver a high-quality program.

How Will the Program Address Our Individual Needs?

This question is especially important if you enter a standardized program. Ask if the program incorporates assessment instruments (e.g., questionnaires) to help you identify the strengths and weaknesses of your relationship. A number of high-quality premarital assessment instruments exist, and many premarital counseling providers administer these assessments to help guide the topics that will be addressed in counseling. If the program incorporates assessments, ensure that the provider received training in how to administer, score, and interpret the instrument. Neither you nor the provider should base serious decisions about the fate of your relationship on a single assessment score.

Assessment instruments provide valuable information for you to discuss with your partner, but no single assessment instrument fully captures all the intricate details of your relationship.

Whether or not your program uses formal assessment tools, consider how well the program will meet your individual needs. If you attend a standardized program, you may have limited time and opportunities to address the unique challenges within your relationship. Standardized programs will teach you general relationship skills, which you can apply to your unique individual circumstances. If you need more individualized attention, ask your provider how she can help you address your unique situation or refer you elsewhere for personalized services. A high-quality premarital counseling provider will be open to receiving your feedback about the program and its ability to meet your needs.

What Is the Timing of the Program? What Is the Cost of the Program?

Again, determine the length and cost of the program. Standardized programs often have an established timeline. Find out if you face any penalties if you or your partner is not able to make it to one or more sessions. This is especially relevant if the program is required. For example, consider a situation in which you and your partner sign up for a program that meets one hour per week for six weeks, and the program is required by your religious institution before you can be married by the clergyperson. What happens if you cannot make it to one session because of an unexpected work crisis? What if your partner gets sick the following week and can't come? Can one partner come alone, or must both partners attend together? These questions point out the importance of learning the attendance requirements of a program. In addition, consider when the program is available to you in relation to your wedding. Six to twelve months before the wedding is the optimal time to participate in premarital counseling. Some programs may even allow nonengaged couples that are considering marriage to participate. Pre-engagement counseling is a wonderful, often underutilized resource that can help many couples decide whether marriage is right for them *before* investing time and energy in planning a wedding.

What Research Supports the Effectiveness of This Program?

Some programs are supported by research, while other programs are marketed without any research supporting their effectiveness. If any research has been done on the program, the provider should be able to summarize the important findings about the effectiveness of the program. She may be able to direct you to resources where you can read more information about research on the program (e.g., journal articles, Web sites, books).

Other programs are based on research findings about marriage development, engaged couples, and adjusting to marriage, even though these programs are sometimes not supported by outcome studies. For these programs, ask the provider to describe the information that was used to develop the program. High-quality research about marital development exists, and this research may form the basis for your premarital counseling program.

Be cautious when the evidence available to support a program is based solely on testimonies of couples or the provider's own impressions of its effectiveness. Testimonies from other couples about the effectiveness of the program may not be applicable to your own relationship (or even worse—they could be fabricated). The provider's own impressions of its effectiveness are likely to be biased by his or her desire to be seen as an effective premarital counselor—which does not mean that the program is not effective; it simply means that you are hearing only one side of the story. If no research is available related to a particular program you are considering, you may also wish to seek out the opinions of other couples—particularly people you know well and trust—related to their experiences within the program.

What Form of Follow-Up Is Available?

You may receive follow-up services (such as additional counseling sessions) later during your engagement or after you are married. Not all programs provide follow-up services, although most providers can direct you to other resources for follow-up services in the community. Follow-up after the wedding is useful and important. Such services offer many benefits to enhance your premarital counseling experience. First, they help you track your progress toward your goals. Second, as new circumstances arise, your relationship will grow and change. Follow-up services help ease these transitions. Third, spending more time with your partner helps you continue to focus on your unique needs, strengths, and problem areas. One premarital counseling provider I surveyed stated, "I would like to see 'end of the first year' counseling instituted. We would have their attention then." This provider's comment reflects the difficulty of truly understanding what marriage is like before you are married. Adjusting to marriage is difficult for everyone. Fortunately, you do not have to go through it alone, so seek continued support from your premarital counseling provider or other resources.

If your program does not include formal follow-up services, create such opportunities on your own. First, make an appointment to meet with your premarital counseling provider after a certain period of time—such as six months or one year. Commit to that appointment as an opportunity to discuss new issues that arise in your relationship.

A second strategy to create a follow-up experience is available to participants in group programs. At the end of the program, arrange with the other couples to get together informally at a later time, especially during everyone's first year of marriage.

Decide on a one-time get-together or a number of informal meetings. For example, you might arrange to meet the first Monday evening of every other month for dinner. Since you shared the premarital counseling experience with these couples, you can form an ongoing informal support group. Your experiences in early marriage will probably be similar to the other couples' experiences. Within your group, share solutions to common problems that arise during the first year of marriage—such as combining finances, making time for each other, and keeping the romance alive.

Third, work with your partner to develop a plan for following up on your own with the lessons you learned in premarital counseling. You won't have the guidance of a practitioner or other couples with this option, so if you choose this option, you should both possess effective communication skills and mutual respect. Develop a plan for how often you want to discuss the progress of your relationship (e.g., once a month), the topics you want to address (e.g., your feelings about the relationship, the strengths of your relationship, and areas for improvement), and signs that you should seek the help of a professional (e.g., facing an impasse with no clear resolution in sight or reaching a major transition point in your marriage).

Continue to work on your relationship after premarital counseling. Be creative and resourceful, and discover the best form of follow-up for you, your partner, and your relationship.

Overview of Selected Premarital Counseling Programs

Here are brief descriptions of some existing premarital counseling programs, along with resources where you can learn more information about each program. This list is not comprehensive, but it provides an introduction to some options that may be available to you. If none of these programs are available in your area, you can identify other resources through a variety of sources: employee assistance programs, community mental health agencies, religious institutions, social service agencies, and mental health professionals.

The Prevention and Relationship Enhancement Program

The Prevention and Relationship Enhancement Program (PREP) was developed by Howard Markman and associates and is the most widely researched program available. PREP is a research-based educational, behavioral approach to marriage preparation that focuses on conflict resolution skills and intimacy promotion. The PREP program incorporates lectures and skill practice. Research shows that PREP increases positive communication, decreases the risk of divorce, increases marital satisfaction, and decreases aggression. One study demonstrated that PREP participants—compared with a control group—demonstrated higher levels of marital satisfaction and less problems three years following participation in the program. PREP is known to be one of the most effective premarital programs available. For more information about PREP, visit the following Web site: *www.prepinc.com.*

The Relationship Enhancement Program

The Relationship Enhancement (RE) program, developed by Bernard Guerney, is an educational approach that aims to eliminate future and present problems. In addition to its use with premarital couples, RE has been adapted for use with a wide range of populations in a number of settings. The programs are structured and can be conducted in group and individual settings. RE programs focus on empathic acceptance of one's partner and behavioral skills. The skills emphasized in premarital RE programs include emotional communication and listening. Research has shown that RE programs are among the most effective premarital preparation programs. Visit the National Institute of Relationship Enhancement Web site at *www.nire.org*, where you can find information about workshops for couples, a directory of RE providers throughout the country, and even a home study course.

Before You Tie the Knot

The Before You Tie the Knot program was developed at the University of Florida Cooperative Extension Service to meet the requirements of legislation by the state government in Florida that encourage engaged couples to receive premarital counseling. The program is available in several counties throughout Florida. This premarital education program presents a four-part curriculum focusing on skills and behavioral interventions. The course is designed for groups of five to ten couples. The four main areas of focus in the course are:

1. Communication—listening and "I" messages

2. Conflict management

3. Financial management

4. Parenting concerns

To find locations of local Cooperative Extension Service offices in Florida, visit *http://extension.ifas.ufl.edu*

Premarital Counseling Program Assesments

The following are examples of some assessments that may be used in a premarital counseling program:

- The PREParation for Marriage Questionnaire (PREP-M), by T. B. Holman, D. Busby, and J. H. Larson (PREParation for Marriage. Provo, UT: Brigham Young University, Marriage Study Consortium, 1989).

- The RELATE Assessment, by T. B. Holman. Premarital Prediction of Marital Quality or Breakup: Research, Theory, and Practice (New York: Kluwer Academic/ Plenum Publishers, 2001).

- The Facilitating Open Couple Communication, Understanding, and Study (FOCCUS), by B. Markey, M. Micheletto, and A. Becker. Facilitating Open Couple Communication, Understanding and Study (FOCCUS) (Omaha: Archdiocese of Omaha, 1985).

- The Premarital Personal and Relationship Evaluation (PREPARE), by D. H. Olson, D. Fournier, and J. Druckman (PREPARE. Minneapolis: PREPARE/ENRICH, 1986).

- The Premarital Inventory Profile (PMIP), by C. K. Burnett and S. L. Sayers. PMI Profile Handbook (Chapel Hill, NC: Intercommunications, 1988).

Conclusion

Many options are available to help you prepare for marriage. The purpose of this chapter was to help you to sort through the options to determine the type of program that is most suitable to your needs. I also hope that this chapter gives you the confidence to have open communication with your premarital counseling provider in order to ensure that your experience meets your unique needs. Because you want the time you spend in premarital counseling to be helpful, consider carefully the type of program that is best for your relationship. In this chapter, you learned important questions to ask to help you gather information and make an informed decision about the provider and format of your program. Find a program that both you and your partner believe will help you strengthen your relationship and create a firm foundation for a solid, satisfying marriage.

Action Plan: A Consumer's Guide to Premarital Counseling

1. Research the types of premarital counseling that are available in your community.

2. Understand the requirements that you face related to premarital counseling through a religious institution or state government.

3. Find a premarital counseling provider who is well qualified and with whom both you will both feel comfortable.

4. Learn about your and your partner's personal preferences for a premarital counseling program: group versus individual couple and standardized versus individualized.

5. Remember to communicate with your provider about your unique needs and make requests to enhance your premarital counseling experience.

Discussion Questions

1. Of the different types of premarital counseling programs, which do you think would be most helpful to you?

2. What type of person do you think would provide you with the best guidance for your marriage?

3. How much time and money are you able and willing to commit to strengthening your marriage?

4. What do you think are your biggest needs in a premarital counseling program?

5. After you complete a premarital counseling program, what would you like to have accomplished?

conclusion
Parting Words

Through reading this book, you have considered many important topics that will affect your marriage. Prepare for marriage now by making positive changes in your life and your relationship. Neither you, nor your partner, nor your relationship needs to be perfect before you marry. Marriages would _never_ succeed if they required perfection. In marriage, you can continue to make changes to enhance your relationship for the rest of your life. When you and your partner love and appreciate each other—including your faults—your marriage becomes a healing, therapeutic relationship. Create a marriage in which you support each other's growth.

In this conclusion, I discuss the limitations and advantages of preparing for marriage. I then discuss the importance of continuing your growth beyond your premarital efforts. Finally, I summarize some of the most important lessons I hope you gained by reading this book.

You Can't Prepare for Everything but You Can Prepare for the Unexpected

You may wonder, "Am I really ready for this?" The answer to this question usually is, "You will never be 100 percent ready for marriage, but you don't need to be!" You will be amazed by how much you learn as you go, as long as you are open to the lessons that marriage will teach you. You'll be better prepared for marriage if you accept and anticipate that you don't know everything. For example, there were many big surprises that awaited me in my own marriage. The major surprise I faced was the difficulty involved in making big decisions together— such as where to live and what we would each try to accomplish in our careers. We are both fiercely independent, and we each have many dreams and plans for what we want to accomplish in life. In the beginning, it was extremely challenging for us to make decisions that took into account the needs of the other person. We could never have been fully prepared for these situations before we married, because these decisions were so significant because we *were* married. Our marriage has grown stronger over the years, which makes these decisions easier for us now.

Preparing for marriage is a useful and valuable endeavor. However, you cannot possibly prepare for everything you will face in marriage. Unexpected challenges will arise throughout your marriage that you could never have predicted. You won't know what your marriage will be like until you are married. Even then, changes will shake up your relationship and your plans. All the premarital preparation in the world will not make you entirely ready to be married. In marriage, expect the unexpected. The best ways to prepare for the unexpected twists of married life are to build a strong, healthy relationship and to develop basic relationship skills (e.g., communication, conflict resolutions, and problem solving). When you develop these resources, your marriage is equipped with tools that you and your partner can use to work together to overcome any test of your relationship. If you have thought carefully about the issues raised in this book, you've gained insights and skills to help you build a satisfying marriage. Even minor efforts toward enhancing your relationship can produce large-scale benefits for personal and relational growth.

Beyond Premarital Counseling

As important as it is to prepare for marriage, you must follow up by continuing to pay attention to and work on your relationship once you marry. Unfortunately, many premarital counseling programs offer no formal follow-up assistance. In fact, society in general often emphasizes preparing for marriage, while other forms of marriage education and counseling are ignored. Too many people only focus on their marriage once it is too late and they are headed for divorce. The notion is that you should prepare for marriage before you enter it, but once you are married, you are on your own. As an example of this paradox, current Florida law provides benefits for couples that attend premarital counseling. Then, divorcing couples with minor children are required to attend a divorce education class. Essentially, these policies pay little to no attention to what happens between premarital counseling and divorce. And, believe me, a *lot* happens between those two experiences!

Seek out help and resources that provide opportunities for you to work on your relationship—even when things are going well. In fact, the best time to work on your relationship is when things are going well. During those times, you'll feel more motivated to work together and create a firm foundation for your relationship. You also have a solid base of support that will allow you to tackle the difficult issues in your marriage. There are countless resources to help you support your marriage—books, seminars, counselors, family life educators, marriage education programs, workshops, and other personal growth experiences.

Remember, though, there are no guarantees in life or in marriage. If anybody or any program ever promises you success in marriage, don't believe it. There are no special secrets or formulas to a good marriage. The keys to a stable, satisfying marriage are available to everyone: long-term commitment, respect, love, relationship skills, fun, and hard work.

Lessons in Love

In this section, I summarize the most important lessons I hope you learned by reading this book.

Marriage can be a rewarding process. Marriage is a big commitment. People often feel scared about what marriage involves. Although marriage involves both positive and negative experiences, the positive experiences can outweigh the negative experiences. You can grow through marriage, and you can support the person you love in his or her growth as well. A number of rewards are available to those couples that remain united in building a strong, supportive marriage.

Marriage is a balance between work and fun. It takes a lot of work to make a marriage succeed. Marriage is not always easy, but it shouldn't always be difficult and boring, either. Make your marriage a fun, enjoyable partnership. When marriage becomes less rewarding, recommit to taking pleasure in your partner and in your relationship.

You can make changes in your life and your relationship to enhance your marriage. You are not destined to repeat the negative relationship patterns from your family-of-origin or your own experiences in past relationships. You can make changes to help your marriage succeed. Recognizing a need to make changes in yourself or your relationship doesn't mean that there is anything wrong with you; it means that you acknowledge that there is always room for growth. Continue moving forward in life, while learning lessons from your past experiences.

Your marriage can change. Your marriage might not turn out to be exactly what you expected. If there is something you do not like about your relationship, you do not need to remain stuck in that pattern for the rest of your relationship. Even couples that seem destined for divorce can manage to shift gears and create a mutually satisfying relationship. You and your partner can work together to create a mutually satisfying marriage, even when things don't go exactly as planned.

The way you use the time leading up to your wedding has an impact on the course of your marriage. Your marriage is a continuation of your premarital relationship. Although marriage is often referred to as a "new beginning" for a couple's relationship, getting married actually signifies a new context for an ongoing relationship. The steps you take now as you prepare for marriage impact the direction your marriage takes in the future. Because this is such an important time in your relationship, make the most of it.

Marriage should be about respect and love for yourself, your partner, and your relationship. Sometimes people fear they will lose their identities or their personal ambitions once they marry. All too many marriages are characterized by dissatisfaction, boredom, and sometimes even abuse. However, the most satisfying marriages allow both partners to fulfill their dreams within the context of a loving, supportive relationship. Ultimately, respecting yourself, respecting your partner, and respecting your relationship are one and the same.

You're on Your Way!

I hope this book has brought to your attention some important considerations to help you prepare for marriage. I hope you have learned skills and information to help you have a better marriage. I hope you have learned the importance of prioritizing and preparing for your marriage. Most of all, I hope you will continue to grow in your relationship throughout your marriage.

By reading this book, you have become more prepared for your marriage, and you and your future spouse spent time and energy getting ready to spend your lives together. I hope you share a wonderful wedding day and it becomes a memory for you to cherish for years to come. Through it all, remember what lies beyond that special day: hard work, lifelong commitment, ups and downs, times of struggle, and times of happiness. Marriage can be wonderful, romantic, and fun. Marriage also involves challenges, heartaches, and balancing your relationship with the other areas of your life. Over time, your marriage has the potential to bring you to a deeper, more passionate experience of yourself, your partner, and your relationship. Trust the process. Marriage is a process through which you will have endless opportunities to grow and share an ever-deepening love with a partner who cares for you so dearly that he or she is willing to love you for the rest of your life.

I wish you the best for a solid, lasting marriage!

Resources

Amato, Paul R., and Alan Booth, *A Generation at Risk: Growing up in an Era of Family Upheaval* (Cambridge, MA: Harvard University Press, 1997).

Amato, Paul R., and Bruce Keith, "Parental Divorce and Adult Well-Being: A Meta-Analysis," *Journal of Marriage and Family* 53 (1991), pp. 43–58.

Amato, Paul R., and Danelle D. DeBoer, "The Transmission of Marital Instability Across Generations: Relationship Skills or Commitment to Marriage?" *Journal of Marriage and Family* 63, no. 4 (2001), pp. 1038–52.

Axelson, John A, *Counseling and Development in a Multicultural Society*, 2nd ed. (Pacific Grove, CA: Brooks/Cole, 1993).

Bach, David, *Smart Couples Finish Rich: Nine Steps to Creating a Rich Future for You and Your Partner* (New York: Broadway Books, 2001).

Barker, Olivia, "Engaged to Marry, Eventually: Couples Want Time to Plan Their Careers as Well as Their Weddings," *USA Today*, 31 December 2003, p. D1.

Becvar, Dorothy S., and Raphael J. Becvar. *Family Therapy: A Systemic Integration* (Botson: Allyn and Bacon, 2000).

Booth, Alan, and John N. Edwards, "Transmission of Marital and Family Quality over the Generations: The Effect of Parental Divorce and Unhappiness," *Journal of Divorce* 13 (1989), pp. 41–57.

Bradt, J. O., "Becoming Parents: Families with Young Children," in *The Changing Family Life Cycle*, 2nd ed., ed. Betty Carter and Monica McGoldrick (Boston: Prentice Hall, 1989), pp. 235–54.

Busby, Dean M, *The Impact of Violence on the Family: Treatment Approaches for Therapists and Other Professionals* (Boston: Allyn and Bacon, 1996).

Carroll, Jason S., and Thomas B. Holman, "Premarital Couple Interactional Processes and Later Marital Quality," in *Premarital Prediction of Marital Quality or Breakup: Research, Theory, and Practice*, ed. Thomas B. Holman (New York: Kluwer Academic/Plenum Publishers, 2001), pp. 141–63.

Carroll, Jason S., and William J. Doherty, "Evaluating the Effectiveness of Premarital Prevention Programs: A Meta-Analytic Review of Outcome Research," *Family Relations* 52 (2003), pp. 105–18.

Christensen, A., and C. L. Heavey, "Interventions for Couples," *Annual Review of Psychology* 50 (1999), pp. 165–90.

Christensen, Teresa M., and Morgan C. Brooks, "Adult Children of Divorce and Intimate Relationships: A Review of the Literature," *Family Journal* 9 (2001), pp. 289–95.

Douglas, D., M. Ferrer, D. Humphries, D. Peacock, and M. Taylor, *Before You Tie the Knot: Leader's Guide* (Gainesville, FL: Cooperative Extension Service, Institute of Food and Agricultural Sciences, University of Florida, 2001).

Ellis, Dave, *Falling Awake* (Rapid City, SD: Breakthrough Enterprise, 2000).

Florida Statutes, Sections 741.0305 and 741.04 (1998), Marriage Preparation and Preservation Act of 1998.

Fraenkel, Peter, Howard Markman, and Scott Stanley, "The Prevention Approach to Relationship Problems," *Sexual and Marital Therapy* 12 (1997), pp. 249–58.

Fukuyama, Mary A., and Todd D. Sevig, *Integrating Spirituality into Multicultural Counseling* (Thousand Oaks, CA: Sage, 1999).

Gabardi, Lisa, and Lee A. Rosén, "Intimate Relationships: College Students from Divorced and Intact Families," in *Divorce and the Next Generation: Effects on Young Adults' Patterns of Intimacy and Expectations for Marriage*, ed. Craig A. Everett (New York: Haworth Press, 1992).

Gardiner, K., M. Fishman, P. P. Nikolov, S. Laud, and A. Glosser, "State Policies to Promote Marriage." United Stated Department of Health and Human Services, 2002. Retrieved 2 May 2007, from: *http://aspe.hhs.gov/hsp/marriage02f/*

Gelfman, D. S., "Adult Children of Divorce and Their Expectations, Attitudes, and Beliefs Regarding Marriage," *Dissertation Abstracts International: Section B: The Sciences and Engineering* 55, (1995), p. 3013.

Glenn, Norval D., and Kathryn B. Kramer, "The Marriages and Divorces of the Children of Divorce," *Journal of Marriage and the Family* 49 (1987), pp. 811–25.

Gottman, John. *Why Marriages Succeed or Fail: And How You Can Make Yours Last* (New York: Simon & Schuster, 1994).

Gottman, John M., *The Marriage Clinic: A Scientifically Based Marital Therapy* (New York: W. W. Norton and Company, 1999).

Greenberg, Jerrold S., *Comprehensive Stress Management* (Boston: McGraw Hill, 2002), p. 198.

Guerney, Jr., Bernard G., *Relationship Enhancement* (San Francisco: Jossey-Bass Publishers, 1979).

Hardin, Jerry D., and Dianne C. Sloan, *Getting Ready for Marriage Workbook* (Nashville, TN: Thomas Nelson Publishers, 1992).

Hochschild, Arlie R., *The Second Shift* (New York: Viking, 1989).

Holdnack, James A., "The Long-Term Effects of Parental Divorce on Family Relationships and the Effects on Adult Children's Self-Concept," in *Divorce and the Next Generation*, ed. Everett, pp. 137–56.

Holmes, Thomas H., and Richard H. Rahe, "The Social Readjustment Rating Scale," *Journal of Psychosomatic Research*, 11 (1967), pp. 213–18.

Holman, Thomas B. *Premarital Prediction of Marital Quality or Breakup: Research, Theory, and Practice* (New York: Kluwer Academic/Plenum Publishers, 2001).

Ivey, Allen E., and Mary Bradford Ivey, *Intentional Interviewing and Counseling: Facilitating Client Development in a Multicultural Society*, 4th ed. (Pacific Grove, CA: Brooks/Cole, 1999).

Jacobson, Neil S., and Andrew Christensen, *Integrative Couple Therapy: Promoting Acceptance and Change* (New York: W. W. Norton & Company, 1996).

Kassin, Saul, *Psychology* (Upper Saddle River, NJ: Prentice Hall, 1998), p. 469.

Kreider, R. M., and J. M. Fields, "Number, Timing, and Duration of Marriages and Divorces: Fall 1996," *Current Population Reports* (Washington, DC: U.S. Census Bureau), pp. 70–80.

Larson, J. H., "'You're My One and Only': Premarital Counseling for Unrealistic Beliefs about Mate Selection," *American Journal of Family Therapy* 20 (1992), pp. 242–53.

Lindahl, Kristin, Mari Clements, and Howard Markman, "The Development of Marriage: A 9-Year Perspective," in *The Developmental Course of Marital Dysfunction*, ed. Thomas N. Bradbury (New York: Cambridge University Press, 1998), pp. 205–36.

Love, Patricia, and Jo Robinson, *Hot Monogamy: Essential Steps to More Passionate, Intimate Lovemaking* (New York: Plume Books, 1994).

Markman, Howard J., Scott M. Stanley, and Susan L. Blumberg, *Fighting for Your Marriage: Positive Steps for Preventing Divorce and Preserving a Lasting Love* (San Francisco: Jossey-Bass, 2001).

Markman, H. J., F. J. Floyd, S. M. Stanley, and R. D. Storaasli, "Prevention of Marital Distress: A Longitudinal Investigation," *Journal of Consulting and Clinical Psychology* 56 (1998), pp. 210–17.

McGoldrick, Monica, and Betty Carter, eds. *The Changing Family Life Cycle*, 2nd ed. (Boston: Prentice Hall, 1989), pp. 209–33.

Mehrabian, Albert. *Nonverbal Communication* (Chicago: Aldine, 1972).

Murray, C. E. "Development of the Couples Resource Map Scales," *Journal of Couple and Relationship Therapy* (forthcoming).

Murray, Christine E., and Thomas L. Murray, "Solution-Focused Premarital Counseling: Helping Couples Build a Vision for Their Marriage," *Journal of Marital and Family Therapy* 30, no. 3 (2004), pp. 349–58.

National Domestic Violence Hotline, at 1-800-799-SAFE (7233) or 1-800-787-3224 (TTY). Visit the Web site at *www.ndvh.org/* for more information on the services and resources the counselors provide.

O'Connell, Bill, *Solution-Focused Therapy* (London: SAGE Publications, 1998).

Olson, D. H., "Marriage in Perspective," in *The Psychology of Marriage: Basic Issues and Applications*, ed. Frank D. Fincham, Thomas N. Bradbury (New York: Guilford Press, 1990), pp. 402–19.

Orman, Suze, *The Road to Wealth: A Comprehensive Guide to Your Money* (New York: Riverhead Books, 2001).

Pinsof, W. M., "The Death of "Til Death Do Us Part": The Transformation of Pair-Bonding in the Twentieth Century," *Family Process* 41 (2002), pp. 135–57.

Ridley, Carl A., and Ingrid E. Sladeczek, "Premarital Relationship Enhancement: Its Effects on Needs to Relate to Others," *Family Relations* 41 (1992), pp. 148–54.

Risch, Gail S., Lisa A. Riley, and Michael G. Lawler, "Problematic Issues in the Early Years of Marriage: Content for Premarital Education," *Journal of Psychology and Theology* 31 (2003), pp. 253–69.

Sayers, S. L., C. S. Kohn, and C. Heavey, "Prevention of Marital Dysfunction: Behavioral Approaches and Beyond," *Clinical Psychology Review* 18 (1998), pp. 713–44.

Schnarch, David, *Passionate Marriage: Keeping Love and Intimacy Alive in Committed Relationships* (New York: Henry Holt and Company, 1997).

Segrin, Chris, and Robin L. Nabi, "Does Television Viewing Cultivate Unrealistic Expectations about Marriage?" *Journal of Communication* (June 2002), pp. 247–63.

Silliman, Benjamin, and Walter R. Schumm, "Improving Practice in Marriage Preparation," *Journal of Sex and Marital Therapy* 25 (1999), pp. 23–43.

Stahmann, Robert F., and William J. Hiebert, *Premarital Counseling* (Lexington, MA: Lexington Books, 1980).

Stanley, Scott M., "Strengthening Marriages and Preventing Divorce: New Directions in Prevention Research," *Family Relations* 44 (1995), pp. 392–402.

Stanley, Scott M., "Making a Case for Premarital Education," *Family Relations* 50 (2001), pp. 272–80.

Stanley, Thomas J., and William D. Danko, *The Millionaire Next Door: The Surprising Secrets of America's Wealthy* (Atlanta, GA: Longstreet Press, 1999).

Stevenson, Michael R., and Black, Kathryn N., *How Divorce Affects Offspring: A Research Approach* (Boulder, CO: Westview Press, 1996).

Straus, Murray A., and Richard J. Gelles, *Physical Violence in American Families* (New Brunswick, NJ: Transaction, 1990).

Sullivan, Kieran T., and Thomas N. Bradbury, "Are Premarital Prevention Programs Reaching Couples at Risk for Marital Dysfunction?" *Journal of Consulting and Clinical Psychology* 65 (1997), pp. 24–30.

Terling-Watt, T., "Explaining Divorce: An Examination of the Relationship between Marital Characteristics and Divorce," *Journal of Divorce and Remarriage* 35 (2001), pp. 125–44.

Thornton, A., and L. Young-DeMarco, "Four Decades of Trends in Attitudes toward Family Issues in the United States: The 1960s through the 1990s," *Journal of Marriage & Family* 63 (2001), pp. 1009–38.

U.S. National Center for Health Statistics, "Reproductive Impairments among Married Couples: United States," National Survey of Family Growth, series 23, no. 11 (1982), Hyattsville, MD: U. S. Department of Health and Human Services.

Waite, Linda J., and Maggie Gallagher, *The Case for Marriage: Why Married People Are Happier, Healthier, and Better off Financially* (New York: Doubleday, 2000).

Wallace, Harvey, *Family Violence: Legal, Medical, and Social Perspectives* (Boston: Allyn and Bacon, 2002).

Wallerstein, Judith S., and Sandra Blakeslee, *The Good Marriage: How and Why Love Lasts* (Boston: Houghton Mifflin, 1995), p. 202.

White, Lynn K., and Alan Booth, "Divorce Over the Life Course," *Journal of Family Issues* 12 (1991), pp. 5–22.

Williams, Lee M., "Premarital Counseling: A Needs Assessment among Engaged Couples," *Contemporary Family Therapy* 14 (1992), pp. 505–18.

Williams, Lee M., and Lisa A. Riley, "An Empirical Approach to Designing Marriage Preparation Programs," *American Journal of Family Therapy* 27 (1999), pp. 271–84.

Willetts-Bloom, Marion C., and Steven L. Nock, "The Effects of Childhood Family Structure and Perceptions of Parents' Marital Happiness and Familial Aspirations," in *Divorce and the Next Generation*, ed. Everett, pp. 3–23.

Working Mother magazine, Web site: *www.workingmother.com*.

Young, Mark E., and Lynn L. Long, *Counseling and Therapy for Couples* (Pacific Grove, CA: Brooks/Cole, 1998).

Index

About the Author

Dr. Christine E. Murray is an assistant professor and coordinator of the couple and family counseling program in the department of counseling and educational development at the University of North Carolina at Greensboro. She received her Ph.D. and master's of education degrees at the University of Florida in Gainesville. In addition, she completed her undergraduate work at Duke University in Durham, North Carolina, where she received dual degrees in sociology and psychology. She is a Licensed Marriage and Family Therapist and Licensed Professional Counselor in North Carolina, as well as a Nationally Certified Counselor. She is a member of the American Counseling Association, the American Association for Marriage and Family Therapy (Clinical Member), and the National Council on Family Relations. Dr. Murray's research interests focus on premarital counseling, intimate partner violence prevention, and strength-based approaches to couple counseling. She is married to Dr. Thomas L. Murray, Jr., LMFT, LPC, NCC. She and her husband live in Greensboro, North Carolina.